FROM COLLEGE STUDENT TO COLLEGE GRADUATE!

The Scoop on Academic Success

Eri Lekura O.D.

For more information, contact the author at:
elekura@umich.edu

ISBN: 979-8-9882459-0-2

Published in 2023.

Printed in the United States of America.

DISCLAIMER

The information and material in this book are based on my experiences and knowledge. However, I am not an expert in study methodology. Therefore, others might have had very different opinions and recommendations from my own.

TABLE OF CONTENTS

PART I
GROUNDWORK

PART II
STRATEGIES

PART III
STUDENT LIFE

ACKNOWLEDGMENTS

I thank God, my family, teachers, role models, friends, and the many others who have helped me throughout my professional journey.

PREFACE

Hindsight is a wonderful thing. Today I know that my life has been a blessing. Looking back at the most challenging times, I realize that they offered lessons to mold me into a better person. Although nothing came easy, I wouldn't change that, because I grew from each experience. I also think luck and God were on my side.

When I have the opportunity to meet and interact with new patients, many of whom are college students, we talk about the schools they are attending, their majors, and some of the challenges they face. I understand some of those challenges and share my experiences and lessons. In addition, I try to offer tidbits of information that might help them better navigate college, mostly because I wish someone had done that for me since I was a first generation college student.

But because eye exams take only 30 minutes, I can share only a minimal amount of information. One day I thought, "What if I write something to share with my young patients some of the lessons I picked up while attending college?" This book is the result.

Designed for use at any time during your studies, readers can cherry-pick through the pages or read the book straight through in just a few hours. It has a three-part structure:

1. The groundwork (Chapters 1-5),
2. The strategies behind studying (Chapters 6-8), and

3. Everything else related to studying and student life (Chapters 9-12).

To put these suggestions in context, they are followed by helpful hints or re-al-world experiences.

To make the most of these resources, I suggest that the reader revisit critical points before starting a school year or taking a big exam. After all, practice makes perfect! The information is not limited to a two- or four-year degree program; it could also apply to any other formal training, whether you're starting technical school or entering a trade.

For teachers, instructors, and professors, I recommend also turning each chapter into a PowerPoint presentation for incoming classes. However, if time is a significant factor (as it frequently is), you might focus on the book's 'meat and potatoes' in Part II.

For parents who want to help their kids, either by getting them up to speed with how to study or by improving their already established study habits, I recommend starting with the chapter topics that you sense might be most needed.

College can be challenging, not only because it's a new experience but also because one's personal life can change at any moment. Still, no matter how tough things seem, we can always take time to find something to be thank-ful for. As with everything in life, I suggest that you take college one day at a time and give your very best effort rather than getting bogged down with regrets. Getting good grades is essential; yet the lessons, experiences, and life knowledge you gain are just as important.

I hope you enjoy reading this book as much as I enjoyed creating it, and I hope it positively impacts you or another student in your life.

- Eri Lekura O.D.

EPIGRAPH

VII

*"People are rewarded in public for what
they've practiced for years in private."*
~ Tony Robbins

PART I

GROUNDWORK

CHAPTER 1

FINANCIAL FOUNDATIONS

"Wealth comes like a turtle and goes away like a gazelle."
~ Arabic Proverb

Regardless of their current financial position, prospective students need to figure out their finances. I believe that students' finances should not dictate what degree they choose to pursue but should be considered more of a 'heads up' on what will happen post-college. For example, student loans are often used without considering how much they will cost long-term. Instead, it would be best to consider interest rate, the loan length, and one's expected net pay after graduation. Let's look at some cost-saving options.

> FINANCES SHOULD NOT DICTATE WHAT DEGREE ONE CHOOSES TO PURSUE BUT SHOULD BE A 'HEADS UP' ON WHAT WILL HAPPEN POST-COLLEGE.

ADVANCED PLACEMENT (AP) COURSES

If you are a high school student reading this book, consider taking as many Advanced Placement (AP) classes as possible. Why? Because each AP class you take means one less class you must pay for in college.

ATTEND A COMMUNITY COLLEGE

In the first couple of years of undergrad, for the majority of majors, students take the same courses to build a common foundation of knowledge. Because the initially-required courses are relatively the same for everyone, students might consider doing the first few years at a community college rather than attending a traditional four-year university because community colleges have lower tuition. Or, if you have committed to a four-year college, consider taking summer courses at a community college near your home.

OTHER POST-SECONDARY TRAINING

I don't think college is the answer to everything, as many other well-respected occupations are available, and a traditional degree is not always necessary for success (Success is a subjective concept unique to an individual.).

For students who think college might not be the right fit, consider going to trade school, doing a formal apprenticeship, or perhaps even doing a stretch of service with the military and exploring their funding options.

COMMUTE TO COLLEGE

Most students, after turning 18, aim to move out and live on campus because they want to get the whole college experience. I think that's a great idea. However, if one has to take out a student loan to pay for an apartment or dorm, it might be wiser to live at home, where your own bills are kept to a minimum. (And many parents or family members will be happy to see you at home.) A little extra time living at home can help you save money in the long run; after you complete a degree program, you can experience life on your own or on campus, if you decide to go back to graduate school.

WORK PART-TIME

I know working part-time, perhaps for minimum wage, might not seem like much, but working *does* help defray personal expenses, and it makes for better time management skills. Additional benefits of working include networking and developing interpersonal skills on the job. It will also help you have some things to put on your resume once you graduate.

TEST OUT OF CLASSES

Many schools offer the opportunity to test out of some courses. These courses are usually pre-requisites, such as computer or government classes (you might have learned this information in high school). Testing out of only one class at a private college can save thousands of dollars; imagine if you multiply that savings by two or three courses!

For more helpful tips, visit The College Investor or Mint₍ₑ₎:

- ▶ **https://thecollegeinvestor.com/22453/save-money-in-college/**
- ▶ **https://mint.intuit.com/blog/relationships-2/how-to-save-money-in-college/#test-out-of**

APPLY FOR SCHOLARSHIPS

According to *Forbes*, an estimated $100 million in scholarship money goes unawarded annually, mainly due to a lack of applicants.[1] So I would encourage looking into scholarships. Scholarships are not just limited to schools; employers, religious institutions, and not-for-profit organizations are just some of the additional sources to look into. Also, check with your parents or

---

1 https://www.forbes.com/sites/markcperna/2021/11/01/100-million-in-scholarship-money-goes-unclaimed-every-year-does-it-have-to/?sh=5fd591833b6f

guardians, loved ones, and friends; essentially, you can look into an infinite number of outlets for new opportunities!

Before starting college, I decided to apply for a highly competitive local scholarship; I had to write about local history that I could only know by talking to someone born pre-1950s (maybe a bit earlier), with nothing based on books or the internet. I did not get the scholarship (even though I put a lot of work into the process). This experience discouraged me from applying for other scholarships, which I now regret; there were so many opportunities out there that I just brushed off! My advice is to keep a positive attitude and don't let one or even a few rejections determine how many scholarships you apply for.

REDUCE THE COST OF MATERIALS

Details about purchasing study supplies are covered in detail in another chapter. Suffice to say that school equipment does not have to be expensive, and neither does clothing, furniture, or other essentials. Explore buying refurbished electronics, perhaps through Facebook Marketplace or Craigslist (taking precautions against scammers, of course!), or visit a local computer repair shop or retail store. Consider secondhand stores or garage sales to find furniture; you might even be able to negotiate a lower price. When it comes to clothing, keep it simple. Do you remember the outfits you wore three months ago, Monday through Friday? (No, right?) As important as it is to dress professionally for job interviews, most clothing does not have to be expensive. Shop off-season locally or online and visit clearance sections.

ON YOUR JOURNEY TO SUCCESS

Here is a simple financial exercise that you can do at any point to get an idea of how much attending school will cost. Consider replacing the years with semesters (e.g., fall, winter, spring, and summer) to make the process easier and/or more precise.

MY ESTIMATED COLLEGE EXPENSES					
Expenses	First Year	Second Year	Third Year	Fourth Year	Total
Transportation					
Health insurance					
Food					
Rent					
School materials					
Tuition/Books					
Personal expenses					
Emergency fund					
Total					

PREPARING FOR CLASS

"One Day or Day One. You decide."
~ *Paulo Coelho*

When I stumbled upon this quote years ago, I took a few moments to reflect. To an extent, we all strive for our goals, whether playing a musical instrument, learning how to dance, or just becoming a better student overall.

As the years progressed, I learned more and more about the importance of preparation. And all of us, to an extent, are enticed to either wait and start preparing later ('One Day') or to take the lead and start the instant we think of our goal ('Day One'). In my experience, studying and preparing for school starts the day you sign up for your college classes, if not earlier! The earlier you prepare, the more successful you are going to be.

Preparing for a class is a lot like playing a competitive sport. The best athletes start preparing well before the season begins. They know that to have an advantage, they need to do something a little extra. In addition, being prepared increases your strategic thinking and mental flexibility as the semester progresses. Although you should not look at your classmates in the course as the competition, it's best to be aware that many classes are competitive, especially if you have ambitions of receiving a more specialized degree.

THE START OF THE SCHOOL YEAR

Each school year is a little different. For example, the material gets more complex, and classes may meet in new buildings or require different online platforms. However, prepping for the school year is a constant.

> **STUDYING AND PREPARING FOR CLASSES STARTS THE DAY YOU REGISTER.**

One or two weeks before school starts:

- Go to sleep early and wake up early in order to be ready for the daily school regimen.

- Buy school supplies such as binders, ink cartridges, etc., in advance, to save time during the school year.

- The week before school starts, look for posted material (such as the syllabus and notes from the professor). Read them as time permits.

- Identify where all classes, labs, and professors' offices are located. Campus maps posted on the school website are invaluable.

- If possible, visit the school and/or attend an orientation to get familiar with the new environment on and off campus. Also determine if you have the online platforms downloaded.

- ▶ Clean up emails, your closet, your dorm, etc., so that valuable study time won't be wasted.

- ▶ Take care of routine doctor appointments such as seeing the dentist, optometrist, or other health professionals. If you take medication, determine how you'll fill prescriptions while at school.

- ▶ Friends are important, make an effort to hang-out with people you might not see in class.

Ultimately you know what's most important in your life, so make time for it.

ON YOUR JOURNEY TO SUCCESS

What else do you usually do before classes start to better prepare for the school year? Note those activities here:

School supplies don't have to be expensive. I managed to save money by buying refurbished electronics such as my laptop. I also asked older students who were done with classes to buy their old books, desks, furnishings, and other equipment. Your cost savings will add up over time.

CREATE A ROUTINE

Often students think that finals week is the hardest, but I'd argue that change can make the first couple of weeks more challenging. Creating a personal daily routine is important to become more efficient and organized, resist any bad study habits, and, most importantly, become more proficient in one's field of study.

MY EXPERIENCE

In most of my academic life, I feel like I took the *laissez-faire* approach. Graduate school was where I tried my best to have a routine. The sole reason? The end of my undergrad program gave me just a hint of the challenges to come in graduate school (and it turned out that I was not wrong).

Before you start the semester, read about or ask about the professors. One website that some students like to use is ratemyprofessors.com. It offers insight into a professor's quality and style of teaching. Keep in mind, though, that students who don't earn a good grade can (and do) target professors for negative reviews. Take everything with a grain of salt because these reviews are subjective, and always never limit yourself to one source of information. For instance, LinkedIn and the school website can provide factual background information on instructor credentials and interests.

Consider asking older students in person about their professors. Questions to ask include:

- How would you describe their teaching style?
- What are some of their expectations?
- Did you understand the instructor?
- How did you study for the class?

Avoid questions such as:

- Is this professor hard? (This depends on the student.)
- Can I receive an easy "A"?

Consider this: If a friend or family recommended a doctor, would you want to see them? Experiences with instructors can function like those referrals.

If you are in a program and there are no other course instructors available, the guidance you receive from websites or other students might help you to better navigate the class. Additionally consider visiting the professor during their office hours and getting to know them face-to-face. Learn what they've done and how they did it.

Questions that you might consider asking the professor:

- From your personal experience lecturing/teaching, what qualities do successful students possess?
- What are your expectations of students?
- What part of the course do students seem to struggle with?
- What resources are available on campus to help master this material?

This information will often be presented on the first day of class or orientation, but sometimes these topics are maybe missed. It's wise to approach your instructor and ask these questions directly. Last, consider sitting in on a lecture and observing the instructor's teaching style, as time permits.

It is only fitting to get to know your teachers and their accomplishments. Through my research, I realized that I had the honor of being taught by some very well-respected professors. I don't think I would have appreciated the opportunity as much if I hadn't discovered their unique backgrounds in their respective fields.

Each week, look at the class schedule, and figure out how each course will shape up (labs, lectures, reading, writing requirements, and so on). By yielding factual information, this type of planning will reduce stress and anxiety, and most importantly, you can make a well-informed decision if something unexpected arises.

Consider reading ahead in your lectures or spend five or ten minutes skimming the next few assigned chapters. Looking ahead will help you make better connections with the material and will allow a quicker grasp of the material when it's presented in class.

Although studying ahead is essential, don't lose focus on what's currently crucial. Find a balance between the two: between short-term and long-term demands.

CHAPTER 3

MATERIALS AND TOOLS

"You cannot mandate productivity; you must provide the tools to let people become their best."

~ Steve Jobs

I cannot overstate the importance of having suitable materials and tools, because access to these resources will decrease the effort needed to study.

Sometimes it's not about working hard or being strategic (although both are important); sometimes, it's about just having the right equipment to get things done. The suitable materials and tools will help you become a better problem solver and more productive long-term; you have to figure out how to make the best of them.

> HAVING SUITABLE MATERIALS AND TOOLS WILL DECREASE THE EFFORT NEEDED TO STUDY.

I grew up in late-twentieth-century, post-communist Eastern Europe. Although I don't necessarily regret my experiences of not having a cellphone or a laptop, I think these tools could have helped me to be more efficient and proficient in studying. Yet, right at your fingertips, whether at home or the college library or student center, students now have access to tools like Microsoft Office, or to the internet, where they are only a few seconds away from useful data and information.

ALARM CLOCK

It's been said that just showing up is 70% of the battle! Using an alarm in the morning is undeniably essential; otherwise, most of us would have difficulty making it to class on time. Both cellphone apps and traditional alarm clocks have advantages and disadvantages, such as accessibility and convenience. Either way, set the time and charge or plug in the device well before going to bed. Nothing beats having peace of mind knowing that music or a tone will sound (or lights will flash!) in the morning no matter what.

I lived at home while I was an undergrad, which meant that even if I overslept, someone in the house would be there to wake me up. But when I moved out and lived alone, there was no one to rely on if I overslept. Furthermore, the consequences were harsh if I missed a class or an exam. Therefore I quickly learned that the best way to have a solid, reliable system to wake up on time constantly was to use both an alarm clock and a cell phone alarm. Since I regularly snoozed my alarm clock, I placed it across my bedroom and raised the volume to the maximum. Then, I would place about three different alarm notifications on my cell phone, so that even if I slept through one, the others would wake me.

BACKPACK ESSENTIALS

As I was finishing my studies, I reflected on how many times I wished I had kept a list of necessary supplies. Although the following list contains items that I believe are important, please consider making a list specific to you, because individual needs can vary according to lifestyle and preferences. Would a star athlete and a new parent, for instance, have the same list?

USE LISTS FOR BETTER CONCENTRATION AND PEACE OF MIND.

In Dr. Lekura's Backpack Essentials

HEALTH CARE KIT

- Hand sanitizer
- Medication for headaches, if needed
- Necessary prescriptions
- Artificial tears (for contact lens wearers)
- Band-Aids
- Medications
- Face mask/face shield

SCHOOL EQUIPMENT

- Extra highlighters and colored pens
- Binder clips
- Heavy duty rubber bands
- Whiteout
- Extra paper
- Extra sticky notes
- Extra flashcards

ELECTRONICS

- Laptop
- Charger (for laptop & cellphone)
- Batteries (AA/AAA)
- Calculator
- Headphones/EarPods
- Recorder
- USB flash drive

OTHER

- Transportation pass
- Tissues
- Chapstick
- Water
- Snacks
- Extra cash or change for parking, tolls, and/or vending machines

List your backpack essentials here:

MY EXPERIENCE

These may seem inconsequential lists, but little things can mean a lot. For example, because of these lists, I was always reassured about remembering critical items on my way out the door. Like your mom's or grandma's purse that seemed to hold anything they may needed, I learned to keep my backpack fully equipped.

EXTRA GEAR

College is a busy time. Always on the go, we can maximize the use of the resources and storage such as a locker or car. Keeping extra gear nearby, such as a change of clothes, shoes, food, equipment, a work uniform, etc., minimizes wasted time.

MY EXPERIENCE

For most of my college years, I drove a 2004 Pontiac Grand Prix GT (I quickly put 160,000 miles on the car). I appreciated the spacious interior and trunk. As I spent more and more time at school, studying or planning events, I essentially kept everything that I needed for the week in my car. Although the car sometimes felt cluttered, it saved me a *lot* of time compared to driving back and forth to my apartment and college.

DAILY CHECKLIST

When in a hurry to leave our house, we can easily forget to take something with us; that's why, right next to the exit door, I suggest that students have a list of all the basics that they need daily. For example:

- ► Coffee or water bottle
- ► Lunch or dorm meal ticket
- ► Homework
- ► Umbrella or outerwear
- ► Keys
- ► Purse or wallet
- ► Media (iPad, Kindle, etc.), if any, for your commute

Still forgetting items? Frame the list (or even write it on the back of your hand!).

What is your daily checklist? Copy or print it and leave it near your front door.

1.

2.

3.

4.

5.

6.

7.

8.

9.

10.

Organization is key to being successful at school, work, and life, so much so that there are countless online articles, magazines, and books on staying organized. The right tools make a difference, especially when learning keeping track of so much new information! Here are my personal suggestions for staying organized during the school year (The same general ideas apply to staying organized using digital folders, notebooks, handouts, or sticky notes.):

Binders/Folders

▶ Use dividers for each lecture or each week.

▶ Keep one binder or folder per class, so you'll know just where to find specific handouts.

▶ Every three-ring binder should have a title on the front, back, and side. Add a table of contents; the same goes for folders.

Notebooks

▶ Like binders or folders, each class should have a dedicated notebook, *no matter how small, and no matter how little you write*. Find a back-to-school sale and buy these in bulk!

▶ Add a title, including course name, course code, professor, and the semester.

- ▸ After class, number the pages to make referencing easier later on.

PowerPoint Slides (PPT)

- ▸ Each PowerPoint presentation can be numbered and dated (for example, "01/01/2023, PPT #3, Exam 1").
- ▸ If they are not numbered already, number all pages or slides.
- ▸ Print single-sided, and/or opt to print multiple slides on each page, because the ink will bleed through a double-sided copy. If you need to write a lot of information for a slide, use the back of the page.

Handouts (H)

- ▸ All handouts should include the professor's name, date, and the related exam (for example, "EXAM 1 – H 1").

Calendar/planners

- ▸ Whether it's a paper or digital calendar, use it correctly. For example, I put all significant events/dates in my calendar app, with reminders, and the less important events/dates in my planner, which I can leave at home.
- ▸ If using a paper calendar, take pictures with a cell phone, if desired, so you can easily access it anywhere.
- ▸ With a computer-based calendar, make sure there is a backup system in case the computer crashes.

▶ Double-check important dates with friends each week. It may feel unnecessary at first, but as schedules get busier during the academic year, a small change can throw things off!

▶ Check your calendar and planner daily, perhaps even a few times a day, to ensure nothing is overlooked.

▶ Track homework time in the school planner, as well as appointments, meetings, and social engagements, to avoid over-crowding the schedule.

Sticky notes

Generally, sticky notes are used for something simple, such as reminders, but they can serve many other purposes, such as:

▶ To separate all book chapters or daily notes (essentially creating tabs).

▶ To highlight essential handouts and book pages.

▶ To mark the beginning and ending points for a reading assignment.

▶ To use the sticky edge as a label for a binder and folder.

▶ To separate flashcards into groups or to label flashcards.

▶ To summarize a particular chapter, handout, or long paragraphs.

▶ Like highlighters, use colors to indicate different meanings (for example, blue or green means reading is complete; pink means needs review).

Binder clips

Think about how many times you wanted to group specific papers and handouts, or you needed to jump back and forth in your book. Clip those important sections during your study period. You can also use binder clips for organizing notebooks, binders, and flashcards.

Rubber bands

Yes, that's right: rubber bands! Rubber bands act as excellent 'object gatherers.' For example, I keep pens and highlighters rolled up in a rubber band for easy access in my backpack, and it helps with not losing them. Use rubber bands to bind your flashcards or split them into groups. They are also a great way to organize power cords and other computer accessories.

> ORGANIZATION IS KEY TO BEING SUCCESSFUL AT SCHOOL, WORK, AND LIFE, AND THE RIGHT TOOLS MAKE A DIFFERENCE.

COMPUTER

Save all your notes, presentations, and handouts on your computer if at all possible, and back it up with an external drive or use a Cloud-based system in order to access the data from a different device.

Each school year should be broken into four folders or levels:

- ▶ (Folder) School year
- ▶ (Subfolder two) Semester
- ▶ (Subfolder three) Class/Subject
- ▶ (Subfolder four) Exams

PLASTIC BINS

When the semester ends:

- ▶ File all paperwork and textbooks in a clear plastic bin. (A bookshelf can easily become disorganized, and bins are easier to move.)
- ▶ Label the bin with the semester or school year, as well as the classes that were covered. So, for example, "Winter 2021: Math 101, English 101, Science 101", etc.
- ▶ Again, buy several bins together, if possible, so they are alike and stackable.

I did not start using plastic bins until later on, in graduate school, when I had to move apartments every year—that is a LOT of packing and unpacking! To simplify and organize my belongings, I got rid of cardboard boxes and bought plastic containers. In a pinch, I could also use the bins for different purposes, such as nightstands and mini study tables.

AUDIO RECORDER

If allowed, consider audio recording every class that's not recorded already. Then, as you record the lecture, you can even write down the time when a particular slide is covered (as some professors like jumping back and forth between slides). Then, when it's time to review your notes, re-listening to a lecture can help fill in any gaps.

Recorders can be a great tool, but don't forget to pay attention to the lectures in real time. Additionally, some professors may prohibit their lectures from being recorded, so always find out the professor's or school's policy before using any recording devices.

WHITEBOARDS

Whiteboards are critical for visual learners and a good investment. Whether made from poster board or an erasable surface, it's a simple but very effective way to stay engaged with course material. Whiteboards can be used for many things, such as:

- ▶ Goals for the day
- ▶ Motivational quotes
- ▶ Scheduling (for work, school, etc.)
- ▶ Problem solving

Make several or update them as your goals change.

WRITING TOOLS

Pen versus pencil (it's a controversial topic)? I believe that a pen should be used when writing, regardless of what we put down. It keeps us focused on not making a mistake because we can't erase it. I also recommend using a black or blue pen and then using a red or purple pen (or another bright color) to highlight/underline. If it's in your budget, consider investing in good pens. The writing comes out better; it looks neater, and it feels better when taking notes during long lectures!

HELPFUL HINT

Use a pencil when writing in a textbook. Ink tends to bleed through the paper.

THE CLOUD PLATFORM

Often offered for free by the school, whether it's Dropbox or Microsoft OneDrive, a Cloud app can be installed on phones, laptops, or desktops; your work is then saved, and you don't have to worry about losing files to a virus or computer malfunction. In addition, you can access schoolwork from anywhere. An alternative to the Cloud platform is a USB. They are inexpensive and have large storage capacities. I encourage students to carry at least two of these external storage devices (see the earlier section on backpack essentials).

We tend to find ourselves more and more often in front of a computer screen. If you log a lot of computer time, consider investing in multiple screens or in one large display screen. If numerous browser windows or files are open, having a large or multiple screens may help with efficiency and will reduce eye strain.

A few additional suggestions:

- Take frequent breaks: follow the 20-20-20 rule. For every 20 minutes on the computer, look away at a distant target (about 20 feet) for 20 seconds.
- Consider using blue light filters to protect your eyes.
- Adjust computer display settings (for example, font size, contrast, brightness).

COMMON SENSE

A little effort in the beginning will make coursework easier in the long run. Now, with your organization complete, enjoy a little break!

CHAPTER 4

ENVIRONMENT AND STUDY SPACE

"You are a product of your environment. So, choose the environment that will best develop you toward your objective. Analyze your life in terms of its environment. Are the things around you helping you toward success —or are they holding you back?"
~ William Clement Stone

William Clement Stone was a famous U.S.-based businessman and philanthropist who believed in always being positive and giving back. He also thought that adversity lays the seeds for success. So, when I first ran into his quote, it made me reflect on the power the environment has on each of us. It's not just the physical environment; I think Stone meant the circumstances or conditions around us as well.

Let's look at some environmental factors that we can influence.

Just getting to class is enough of a challenge, yet if one wants to excel, taking additional steps to stand out from the crowd can help. Sitting in front during a lecture offers three advantages:

- Better access to the professor
- Less distraction from classmates
- A better view of the material

On exam day, this helps in many different ways, including:

- Quicker access to the professor for questions to clarify exam questions.
- Depending on how the exam is distributed, more time to finish the exam than if you sat in the back of the hall.
- Option to easily move in and out of the classroom (if one needs to use the restroom or has an emergency).

For students with mobility challenges who might prefer to sit along an aisle or in the back of the room for easier access to the exit, consider:

- Using an audio recorder (see Chapter 3).
- Looking for note-taking assistance.
- Request extra time to complete an exam or a digital format.

Because I would stay up late to study, I had a hard time waking up in the morning and arriving early enough to sit in the front of a lecture hall. I would choose a seat that was strategically important. For example, I preferred a seat near the end of an aisle. It made it easy to move in and out, plus I didn't block anyone's view if I arrived late.

STUDY AREAS AND SPACE

Consider identifying three to five study areas, such as libraries, quiet coffee shops, schools, parks, your kitchen table, etc. Using a variety of spaces make studying more interesting and less routine. Organize and clean the space first. When learning at home, have a designated study room, and try *not* to use the bedroom. (Ideally, the bedroom should be used only for relaxation and a sound sleep.)

If away from home, try to pick a study area that offers seven features:

- A restroom nearby (within walking distance)
- Free internet
- Free parking or easy public transportation accessibility
- A safe environment
- Lots of study space

- ▶ Lots of electrical outlets
- ▶ Privacy (more about this shortly)

Consider not sharing a secret (quiet) study spot with classmates. When one finds a true gem, it's better to hold on to it.

> **FOR PRIVACY, TRY NOT TO SHARE A SECRET (QUIET) STUDY SPOT WITH CLASSMATES. WHEN ONE FINDS A TRUE GEM, IT'S BETTER TO HOLD ON TO IT.**

ON YOUR JOURNEY TO SUCCESS

List five spaces where you like to study and put "yes" or "no" next to each place if they meet all seven of the recommended features listed in the previous section. This will filter the best study spots and indicate whether it's time to reconsider some of your current study areas.

1.

2.

3.

4.

5.

MY EXPERIENCE

While at the University of Michigan-Dearborn (UMD) campus, I sometimes left all my belongings unattended for hours. Yet I understood over time that the UMD campus was unique because it had a tight-knit community where theft rarely occurred. This is not the case with all campuses. Therefore, be cautious before leaving anything behind, and even in a limited-access area, *never leave a personal ID, cash, or any valuable equipment unattended.*

Remove potential distractions *before* they become actual distractions.

Cellphone

▶ Consider turning your phone off. To be safe, text your location to a loved one first. Another option is to consider placing your cellphone on mute and putting it out of sight (the inside of a backpack or inside a drawer).

▶ Check messages only when taking a break.

▶ Erase any non-essential apps. Some apps are more valuable than others, and new ones are constantly being developed and marketed to distract us, so don't install what you don't need.

Social media

▶ Consider deactivating your accounts unless they are used to communicate with classmates, such as a study group. In that case, consider creating a secondary account to share only with that group.

People

▶ When studying, limit interactions with others as much as possible. Otherwise, there is a risk of unnecessary socializing, problems, and other distractions.

Other helpful hints:

- Background noises: consider using noise-cancelling headphones (also see the specific suggestions about dealing with noise).
- Have everything you need or might need close by (snacks, printer, books) before you begin.

MY EXPERIENCE

For most of my college experience, Facebook was the most popular social media platform. I spent a lot of time on it as an undergrad. As my schedule got busier, I realized that I needed to make better use of my time and limited my activity on Facebook. I would deactivate my account for months, but later realized that I was missing a big part of online conversations. To address this problem, I created a second, temporary account. Through this account, I was part of the online course groups, where I could still interact, but was not fully attached to the rest of the social media platform.

USE PROPER LIGHTING

Lighting plays a big part in our brain's ability to focus, affecting our mood, eye strain, headaches, and energy. Different types of lighting are designed for specific tasks. Research the type of lighting that works best for you.

<u>Three Lighting Options for Studying</u>

- ▶ **Focusing**: Task lighting provides increased light for specific tasks such as studying on a desk (for example, a desk lamp).

- ▶ **General studying and reviewing**: "Showtime" lighting is how I describe turning all the room lights on.

- ▶ **Reading, writing, and group study**: Natural lighting, also called sunlight. (I believe it is the best lighting type, because the light spectrum doesn't damage or hurt your eyes.)

BACKGROUND SOUNDS: WHITE OR PINK NOISE

While studying, we often have to deal with three or four distracting background noises at once. To block them and improve focus, I used white noise. Some examples of convenient white noise sounds are a whirring fan or a humming air conditioner (even radio static at low volume can work). You might be familiar with another noise type: pink noise. Some examples of these pleasant sounds are waves crashing on the beach or falling rain.

Although I do not, some prefer to study with regular ambient noise, like music or the din of a bustling café, to stay alert. I encourage you to try each of these to see which works best for you.

USE AVAILABLE RESOURCES

Most schools provide math and writing centers, as well as free tutoring. Scout them out and use them frequently. All these resources are there for *you*, the student. Don't hesitate on using them. Additional resources might include:

- Academic advisors
- Counselors
- Food co-ops or food pantries
- Internship placements
- Libraries
- Medical clinics

Contact the student services office and/or the school's student center for more information.

MY EXPERIENCE

Universities don't always adequately explain their services, yet I don't believe the responsibility falls solely on the institution but also on the individual student. Students, too, can neglect to meet with their counselors or talk to their professors about resources. I often learned about the services provided through older friends and sheer luck.

USE YOUR CAR AND OTHER SPACES

So, it's finals week: the library is packed, the coffee shops are full of people, and home is too distracting. Where to go? Consider studying in your car. We've already seen that the car can be a great mobile storage space, and because you can park (legally) almost anywhere, it easily becomes a quiet place to learn.

For students who don't have a car, consider the following alternatives:

- ▶ Consider borrowing a friend's car for the day or just a few hours to find a quiet place to focus.

- ▶ Consider renting a car for the day; if it's a holiday weekend and car rentals are expensive, consider renting from places like U-Haul and picking up a small pickup truck. Bring a quiet friend along!

- ▶ Is a friend going out of town? Become their favorite house-sitter or pet-walking service.

- ▶ What about your house of worship? Their offices might be unused during certain times of the week.

- ▶ Community centers often designate space for study.

- ▶ If you absolutely need a quiet desk and time alone to write or study, consider renting a room via Airbnb or even a motel or hotel room. Look at online discount booking sites. Booking a room overnight can be expensive, but, just like education, it's an investment in your future.

USE THE SCHOOL'S DESK

My personal opinion is that one way to reduce anxiety is to study at school, at the same desk and in the specific area where the test will be held. This will help build confidence. Tell yourself, "I was just here a few days ago reading about this material," being reassured that the exam material was covered while you studied.

In graduate school, we had access to our optometry building 24/7, but that's not always the case while in undergrad. Still, students could ask the instructor if they could study in a specific lecture hall or classroom where they will be tested. In addition, some professors might be inclined to let students learn there, understanding that anxiety can negatively affect exam scores.

USE YOUR SENSE OF SMELL

Some students enjoy studying using different scented candles, lotions, or wildflower scents. Mint is thought to be stimulating, for example. Try using different scents for various exams. It might help you feel relaxed and refreshed. Could relating a specific smell to a particular topic help with recall? Something to consider!

CONSIDER THE TEMPERATURE

If studying at home, ensure the room temperature is not too warm. Or match the temperature of the library or school. Also, providing good air circulation keeps you focused and alert.

When I knew that I would be studying for at least a couple of hours, I kept the window cracked, open just enough that even if it was cold outside, it brought in some much-needed fresh air. During summer, although the A/C was on, I would do the same thing, or keep a fan in the room to constantly circulate the air, so it didn't feel too damp.

Now, use a whiteboard or bulletin board to post images of the study resources that work best for you.

CHAPTER 5

NOTE-TAKING

"The faintest ink is more powerful
than the strongest memory."
~ Unknown

While writing this book, I reflected on one skill I improved on as my college years progressed: note-taking. Note-taking is essential because notes often contain materials and ideas found nowhere else. Consider class notes similar to a rare baseball card or painting; they're invaluable.

Also, while writing or typing notes, students study and think about what to record. In addition, taking good notes is not only a skill applied in school but a lifelong one that will improve as we gain experience.

Finally, as we age, our memory is often not as sharp as it was when we were younger. Yet our list of adult responsibilities and tasks keeps on growing! Thus, the better note-taker one becomes, the easier it will be to juggle those multiple roles.

I understand that we are relying more and more on our laptops, tablets, iPads, and other tools for taking notes, and for good reason. They are practical, light, and create documents accessible anywhere with the proper storage or Cloud-based system. Thus, it is good to know how to customize the notebooks you purchased earlier (see Chapter 3).

Customization Tips

- The first few pages of your notebook should have a key and table of contents. The table of contents serves two purposes: it offers an overview of what's in the notebook, and it provides a framework for the organization for the notes. It will allow you to go directly to specific topics.

- Maintain a key to all the acronyms, symbols, or words used and their meanings, which will help when you revisit your notes and need clarification.

- All lectures should be titled and dated.

- Leave space between different chapters or sets of lecture notes in case you decide to go back later and add updates.

During my third year in optometry school, students had to take full-time classes with lab work. In addition, we saw individual patients each week in the clinic and were studying for board examinations (essentially a review of everything learned in optometry school and some aspects since undergrad). This was when I became obsessed with the organization and customization of my notebooks. Part I of the board exams was called Applied Basic Science. It was known as the hardest of the three boards, partly because it covered many topics and was lengthy (roughly an eight-hour exam). You can imagine how much studying I did and how much material I had to review.

WHEN STUDYING FOR A BIG EXAM, EVERY MINUTE COUNTS! DON'T WASTE TIME FLIPPING THROUGH NOTES, LOOKING FOR A SPECIFIC WORD OR TOPIC: GET ORGANIZED!

The more organized our notes are, the more efficient our studying will be. Most students enjoy taking notes using the outline method; essentially, this format uses bullet points (very similar to how I have organized these chapters). Or, use the mind-mapping method, which is a sort of flowchart of ideas.

When writing our notes by hand (versus on a computer), ask these three questions:

- ▶ Could I read this after one year?
- ▶ Could I understand this after one year?
- ▶ Is there enough space to add more material later?

HELPFUL HINT

Plenty of videos are available online to help with organizing our notes correctly, but many are very detail-oriented. I don't think that's beneficial to the average student. Therefore be cautious about over-complicating this process. Unless we publish our notes, no one else needs to understand them other than ourselves.

Try out the following two formats. Using materials from a recent class or a section of a textbook, take notes using the sample outline or sample mind-map charts, or look online for other ideas that fit your thinking style.

[Class, Chapter, Date]

Sample Outline

I. Topic

- ▶ Point one:
- ▶ Point two:
- ▶ Point three:

II. Topic

- ▶ Point one:
- ▶ Point two:
- ▶ Point three:

Sample Mind Maps

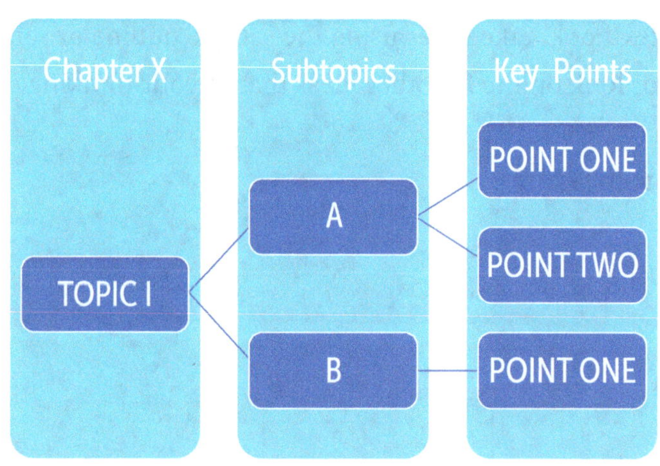

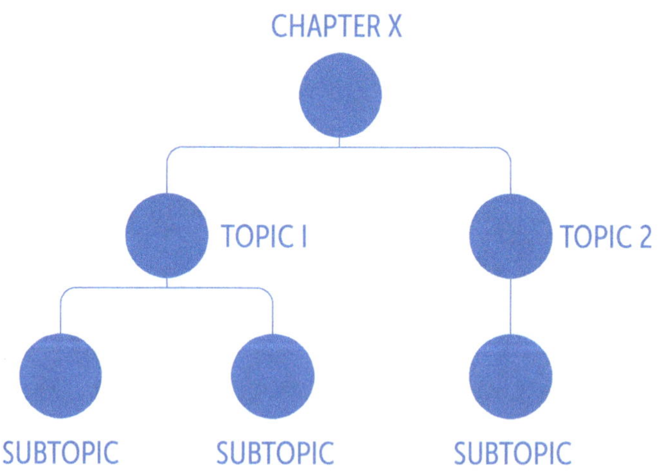

ADD CITATIONS OR OTHER REFERENCES

Sometimes a professor jumps between different books and presentations. So, naturally, referencing the source will help. A reference can be a page number, a book title, or a date—anything to make cross-referencing easier.

REVIEW YOUR CLASS NOTES

We can all get to the point where our notes seem scattered. Perhaps the professor is just skipping around, and we can't understand a thing. As in the previous exercise, it's wise to go back and review or even **rewrite** them. But keep the original, just in case.

MY EXPERIENCE

My handwriting is not the greatest. Many of my co-workers describe it as typical "doctor's handwriting." I knew this early on, so I would rewrite my notes. Although rewriting notes can be time-consuming, it was beneficial in the long run. I retained the information by, in effect, studying the material as I rewrote it.

WRITING VERSUS TYPING

Writing by hand, in general, improves recall, perhaps because we are more engaged with the material. Some exceptions when typing is preferable to handwriting are:

- ▶ When your professor is speaking quickly, and you know that you can type faster than you can write long-hand.

- ▶ The lecture is in PDF or PowerPoint format, and the file is open on your computer.

- ▶ The presentation material is disorganized or doesn't follow the actual lecture.

In these cases, typing can save a great deal of time. As technology progresses and computer-based learning becomes more common, it might be the most straightforward option.

USE SYMBOLS AND ABBREVIATIONS

Instructors and students love using both symbols and abbreviations; when used correctly, they can save time. Some of my favorite symbols and abbreviations that I used are listed here and might be added to your notebook key:

<table>
<tr><td>

Dr. Lekura's Symbols

(?) – Should I know this? or I don't understand this

Ⓚ – *I need to know*

Ⓔ – *It's on the exam/or just exam*

(Q) – *Question*

(A) – *Answer*

>/< – *Greater than or less than*

</td><td>

Dr. Lekura's Abbreviations

b/c – because

w/o – *without*

max – *maximum*

PPT – *PowerPoint*

H – *handout*

</td></tr>
</table>

You, too, can create/borrow customized symbols and abbreviations; just remember their meaning with a key. You can also combine symbols with abbreviations or symbols with symbols, etc. For example:

(?)Ⓔ – *Will this be on the exam? or Should I know this for the exam?*

b/c ⓀⒺ – *Because I need to know for the exam*

What are some symbols and abbreviations that you like to use?

<table>
<tr><td>List of symbols:</td><td>List of abbreviations:</td></tr>
<tr><td>

</td><td></td></tr>
</table>

TRACK DOWN EXTRA NOTES

Have you ever watched a movie with a close friend and come up with two different conclusions about what the director was trying to convey? Like analyzing movies, art, or anything else, even if you and your friend share many opinions, you could differ in how you perceive the world.

School, specific classes, or certain topics that can be challenging might also be better understood from different angles. Ask to borrow your classmate's notes if you don't understand a topic or lecture. Classmates might pick up on the information that you disregarded as unnecessary, giving a different perspective on the material. If your classmates do not want to provide their notes, see if you can find someone who passed the class previously, and ask if they are willing to share their old notes. If you still can't find anyone, see if the textbook comes with any outlines or PowerPoint slides online. (If you have a text handy, take a moment now to check the publisher's website.)

MY EXPERIENCE

I first applied this study tip when pledging to join my fraternity Delta Sigma Phi. It was the winter semester of 2010, and on top of spending a lot of time pledging, I had a full plate with classes and labs, volunteering, and working two or three days a week. I was also an officer with three other student organizations, and of course, there were responsibilities to family and friends.

As the pledging process got more challenging, I had less and less time to study, and I found myself walking a tightrope for one class: biology. To prepare for an exam, besides my study guides, I asked a friend to borrow theirs because I knew I would forget something important to study.

SHOW YOUR STEPS

When watching a video about cooking, drawing, and so on, have you ever realized the chef or artist skipped a few steps (known as the "trade secret")? No matter how much you slowed the video, a few steps were missing. Well, many subjects in school are like that; math is a perfect example, because we tend to do a lot of the "solving" in our heads:

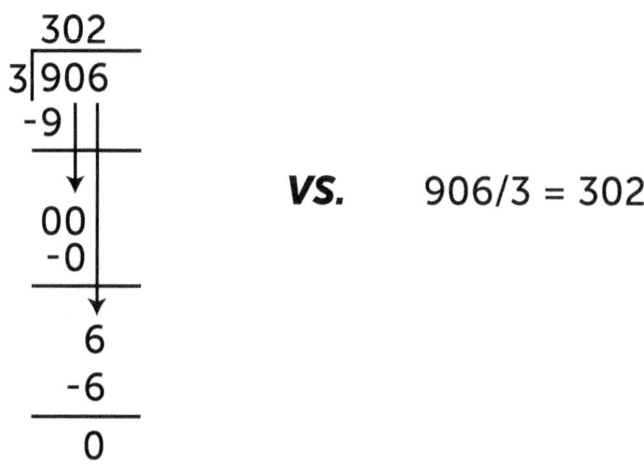

Revisiting their notes, students may realize that they forgot how to do the problem, and that there are no steps to direct them. That is why it is essential to *show all steps in your notes*. Showing all steps when solving a problem adds very little extra time when doing homework, and it helps a *ton* when studying or revisiting a topic. It will also make things much easier to understand! If there isn't time to show all the steps, at least note that steps were skipped.

In General Chemistry, as I progressed through the class, I remember feeling more comfortable with the material. I decided to skip a few steps (for example, when doing oxidation-reduction reaction problems). Long story short, when the final exam came and I started reviewing the material, I realized that I had forgotten a few things. Thus, I ultimately struggled more than necessary.

PICTURES AND SCREENSHOTS

From time to time, professors will quickly write and then erase what's on the board. If so, take a picture of the writing and make time to listen in class and to study the image later. Screenshots will also help with small images from PowerPoint or PDF presentations. For example, if an image is microscopic, simply take a screenshot and zoom in to see it more clearly. If none of these steps will work for you, ask the professor for a detailed explanation of the visuals or if a narrated video is available elsewhere.

As discussed in the section on audio recordings, *always ask the professor* for permission before taking a picture or a screenshot, as it might go against their policies or the policies of the school. Students with disabilities, language barriers, special needs, or even transportation challenges might choose to work with their school's office for accommodation or to contact the professor directly about their circumstances. Exceptions can often be made to specific policies.

***

Congratulations on reading Part I! In Part II, we'll explore strategies for conquering your coursework.

STRATEGIES

CHAPTER 6

STRATEGIES FOR STUDYING AT SCHOOL

"The bad news is time flies. The good news is you're the pilot."
~ Michael Altshuler

We are constantly bombarded with the things we must do in a day. For some students, it's finding a babysitter for their child; for others, it's trying to pick up a few extra hours at work to pay for a class; thus, we think that the only time to study is what we have left after we finish all other tasks. The good news is that one can apply many strategies in class or between classes to learn, understand the material, and prepare for an exam.

Think of the time in school as the *most valuable time* to study. Just attending class *is* studying, as you are acquiring new information. Whatever comes after school is just extra time to tune into what was learned in class.

> **THINK OF THE TIME IN SCHOOL AS THE MOST VALUABLE TIME TO STUDY.**

It's important to attend classes in person whenever possible (and, at the very least, when required). I understand that specific lectures can be monotonous, yet by attending class, students have the opportunity to engage with the material, to build relationships with classmates and instructors, and, most importantly, to learn without distractions. Students can become involved in discussions and dialogue, paying attention to verbal and nonverbal cues, all by attending class.

For online classes, keep these tips in mind:

- Identify a good space for your computer. Think about a quiet place, where you will not be interrupted, and where there is a strong internet connection. If there is no such place at home, consider a coffee shop or library that offers free internet.

- Become familiar with the features that the course video platform offers. Play around with the features and ask the instructor to explain if something seems unfamiliar. Remember, though, that lecture time is tight.

- If you feel at all uncomfortable with online platforms, look on the internet, YouTube, or the college website for tutorials on how to use the features.

- Consider muting your own microphone if it is not required.

- Think through any question or comment *before* asking. Since it's an online class, the posts will likely remain in the lecture recording. Or wait until the class is over, and contact the professor later.

ASK QUESTIONS

Asking questions is a great way to double-check one's thought process! Asking questions can happen in four different ways, and I recommend to utilize all four, especially with more complex subjects.

- ▶ Ask questions during the lecture.

- ▶ Ask the professor questions right after class, when the material is still fresh in your mind.

- ▶ Office hours: Spend as much time with the professor as needed, but go in prepared, knowing precisely where your struggles are. It's not the professor's job to determine where you need help. Respect their time, and use it wisely.

- ▶ On the day(s) before the exam, email any remaining specific questions. Don't hesitate to ask even last-minute questions, because it could significantly affect a test grade.

When asking a question, keep in mind:

- ► It needs to be specific; figure out what is bothering you and what area(s) you do not understand.

- ► Use an example when asking a question to make sure it's clear.

- ► Have the questions ready, jotting them down before lecture or office hours, so you do not waste time reviewing your notes to find them.

- ► Bring notes and books along when talking to the professor.

MY EXPERIENCE

Both in undergrad and graduate school, last-minute questions had a significant impact on my grades. In addition, they helped clarify topics I wasn't too clear on, which also helped me do well on exams.

ASK "WHY?"

Whether writing a paper, studying physics, or learning a foreign language, one must constantly be asking, "Why?" Why does it occur like that? Why did they write it that way? Why do I need to know? By asking why you are putting purpose over the process that you are involved in.

Asking "Why?" forms a logical pattern that makes a topic easier to understand. It's also important for feeding and cultivating one's curiosity as well as providing a greater meaning in context. Perhaps it's not an innate part of our personality, but we must step up and ask additional questions about anything that's unclear.

MY EXPERIENCE

Two of my good friends are always asking, "Why?" Sometimes they overdo it, yet I think we need people like that in our lives, the ones asking the waiter all the specific questions about the menu (perhaps getting on their nerves!). One of these two friends used to work at a car dealership. When I was car shopping, I asked him to tag along for a second opinion.

At the dealership, as the salesman was making his speech and sales pitch, my friend started asking questions I had never considered, citing the *Kelly Blue Book* price and a review of the car's accident report history. Although the used vehicle was reported online as having a "minor fender bender," after my friend asked for the report, it turned out to be more than just that. This is why it's important to understand what purpose is driving the process.

Review sessions are important for last-minute questions. In addition, professors will sometimes give out precise information about the exam. If you can't attend a review session due to your schedule, ask a friend to see what was discussed and if you can borrow their notes.

FREQUENTLY CHECK YOUR GRADES

Students need to check their grades often for many different reasons, such as:

- ▶ Deciding what class needs to be prioritized.
- ▶ Figuring out which exams are a priority.
- ▶ Making sure the correct grade was recorded (professors and software can make mistakes).
- ▶ Understanding where the grade stands in the class (top versus bottom).

HELPFUL HINT

Find the time that works for you to check a grade. Don't feel obligated to check a test score immediately, as the outcome can impact your mood or might affect how you do on a consecutive exam. If you are pleased with the grade, celebrate. If not, see where you need more focused study, then take time out for yourself. Pause now to consider when you might check this week's grades.

TEACH OTHERS

Helping other students provides reassurance that we know the information well. If we struggle to teach or explain the subject matter, perhaps we cannot understand the material from different angles, or perhaps we don't understand the material well overall. If you feel confident enough, though, and time permits, consider reviewing the material with a friend and perhaps teaching them what you have learned.

Teaching others can go a long way, and it doesn't have to be limited to a peer group. For example, I helped out many friends who struggled with math. Although I enjoyed helping them, it also helped *me*, refreshing my memory on that subject.

SET MORE GOALS THAN YOU CAN ACHIEVE

We all set specific goals in life, whether financial, health-related, personal, or professional. When it comes to education and learning, we want to have more goals than we feel comfortable with, because our big goals stretch what we believe is possible.

Setting goals can help us stay active, focused, and prepared. For example, some goals could be receiving better grades in all our classes, or becoming a better writer, or something as simple as finishing our homework on time. It's okay if we cannot accomplish all the objectives. The important part is that we constantly work towards them.

> IT'S OKAY IF WE CANNOT ACCOMPLISH ALL THE GOALS. THE IMPORTANT PART IS THAT WE CONSTANTLY WORK TOWARDS THEM.

For even greater progress, always take an additional step with homework. For example, visit the writing center for feedback on a draft assignment, or ask a friend to review your paper. If unsure about the solutions to assigned problems, double-check with a few friends. This extra effort can mean the difference between a "B" and an "A."

Consider taking additional steps *if there is plenty of time to turn in an assignment.* If short on time, there is no guarantee that someone will be willing to double-check one's work. Use the built-in spell-check and grammar-check feature in your word processing application or find a free app online. That can review your work and hopefully catch any mistakes.

Learn how to divide and conquer! When you have a big exam, project, or presentation coming up and are running out of time, it's okay to ask a friend, classmate, or family member to help out. Whether it's taking notes from a recording or splitting up the project work, be sure to reciprocate.

Although it's been some years since I finished college, I remember one class where my classmates and I worked as a team to do as well as we could: microbiology. The professor was very inconsistent in presenting the material, jumping between PowerPoint slides and spending time on a slide that might contain only a few words. Students who did not record his lectures were at a big disadvantage in the exam, because he would verbally explain so much of what he wanted you to know. In order to listen to all the hours of audio, my classmates and I decided to split up the work among us and then share notes, which worked wonderfully.

Whether reading, note-taking, using flashcards, or taking practice exams, all these steps are necessary for us to succeed. Resist the urge to skip a step when you're not feeling like it or when it seems unnecessary. As time goes on, students will become much more efficient with the cycle and continue to build confidence, because, as the saying goes, practice makes perfect.

When pressed for time, focus on the step of the study cycle that has created the most success so far. If the flashcards worked, focus on those; if reading the texts worked better, focus on the book. Even though it's essential to follow the study cycle, you can pick what has worked best for you. The cycle routine will also help you get back on track when the unexpected happens.

PRINT WHAT YOU CANNOT RELIABLY SAVE

Having a physical copy will help with easy access to the school material. Remember that the material from websites won't always be accessible online, even in an online class. If you can't print the material, consider saving it to a computer or a USB device. If you don't have access to a printer, many universities and public libraries allow you to print for free or at a reduced cost.

DRESS PROPERLY

Unfortunately, we sometimes put too much thought into how we look—or on the other extreme, perhaps no thought at all! For example, while studying, wearing pajamas and sweats doesn't lift our mood. Consider instead, dressing appropriately (revisit the many ideas in this book for how to do that without breaking your budget). This goes both for attending school or studying solo. It simultaneously signals respect for one's professors and self-respect. If you're known for running late, try to have an outfit ready the day before.

RED FLAG SITUATIONS

Special circumstances require special attentiveness. Here are my suggestions for how to deal with them:

- ▶ A professor or friend might say this exam is "easy" or, "Don't worry about it." This could be accurate, but often it's not. Always prepare as if it will be a challenging exam.

- ▶ If a PowerPoint slide contains very little detail, that does not mean it's not important.

- ▶ If the professor spends a lot of time on one slide, **pay attention**, even if the topic doesn't seem relevant at the time.

- ▶ If the professor skips a PowerPoint slide, mention it. It could have been either accidental or not, so it's best to clarify.

- ▶ Sample problems: If a professor solves a sample problem, they are likely solving a manageable-to-easy problem to get started. This is a perfect opportunity to ask the professor, "What if." For instance, what if one variable or result were to change? They might have time to solve another sample problem and provide an extra example.

- ▶ Don't assume all classes take an equal amount of work. For example, sometimes 'easy' concepts or 'easy' lessons will actually take longer to study. I took an intro-level anthropology class that seemed like it would be relatively easy, but it wasn't. I spent more time doing homework in that class than in any other in my first few years of undergrad.

- ▶ Guest lecturers: Take notes on what they are presenting and ask if you could have a copy of their notes, too, as they always come in handy.

- ▶ Be cautious of what I call the 'PowerPoint outline illusion.' Some professors present the PowerPoint with a nice outline, but as you proceed, the slides don't follow the outline. Unintentionally, they might have moved the original slide order or adjusted the lecture for some reason, but never updated the outline.

We tend to forget how long a day lasts. With 24 hours ahead, students can often figure out how to be more efficient. For example, I became more efficient by using class breaks to study. I would sometimes have a small snack during class; that way, I could use meal breaks to learn or review material. (Some professors allow snacking during lecture, and others do not, so it's best to check.)

Every minute saved adds up. Using 25-minute breaks for studying each day, over the course of a five-day school week, totaled about two hours of study. If you commute, take advantage of the drive or time on public transportation. Replaying recorded lectures is an excellent way to refresh the material.

HELPFUL HINT

By taking advantage of the 'in-between' time, by no means do I mean doing this every day. On the contrary, allowing downtime to recharge for the next class is very important. In semesters or weeks that are jam-packed with stuff, we just need to look for those little pockets of time to rest or study.

Struggling in school or with a particular subject? Ask a successful, well-rested classmate what they did to study or prepare. We might automatically assume that our friends and peers are all doing the same things, yet there are times when they are not. Asking your classmate for suggestions does not make you look bad; if anything, it shows that you respect their intelligence. You might even discover something new.

CHAPTER 7

RETAINING WHAT YOU'VE LEARNED

*"Strategy without tactics is the slowest route to victory.
Tactics without strategy are the noise before defeat."*
~ Sun Tzu

This chapter represents one tactic, one of the bigger pieces of the puzzle we are trying to solve, but it is not the whole puzzle. Don't focus only on this information without visiting and understanding the other chapters as well, to get a broader context.

MY EXPERIENCE

Magnus Carlsen a chess Grandmaster claims to see at least 15 or 20 moves ahead. As a chess player myself, I can attest that it requires a *lot* of strategizing! Just like great chess players, students can strategize when studying.

By noticing winning strategies, students can be proactive about the future, where decisions have been well thought out.

USE ALL FOUR TYPES OF LEARNING

Over the years, researchers from distinguished figures like Neil Fleming have proposed four learning styles or a mixture of the four: visual, auditory, reading/writing, and kinesthetic (hands-on). Ideally, studying includes all four types. Like many people, I am a visual learner, but I also integrate other types into my study routine. Whether reading, writing, listening, or practicing the information, different parts of the brain are engaged, and that helps tremendously with long-term memory. For more information, explore this website:

What's Your Learning Style? 20 Questions (2022)

http://www.educationplanner.org/students/self-assessments/learning-styles-quiz.shtml

We all learn a little bit differently. Think about what timing works for you. If you enjoy studying in the morning and see success, do that. If you are a night owl and see success that way, then learn at night. This choice isn't permanent and can change from class to class and semester to semester.

MY EXPERIENCE

It took me some time to figure out my best time for studying. It turned out that I was a night owl. Even if I had class at eight a.m. or at eight p.m., I didn't mind being up until two or three that morning studying. But I did take an afternoon nap (for about an hour) in order to stay up late.

STUDY WELL IN ADVANCE

A common consensus on how many hours we should spend *per lecture* is two to three hours of studying. For example, if we have a one-hour class four times a week, we should spend between 8 and 12 hours studying a week for that particular course. For most exams, we need one or two weeks to review all the material. Although it might seem excessive, this allows enough time to prepare even if something unexpected happens to our schedule. Additionally it's best to plan for the unexpected.

EXPECT THE UNEXPECTED.

Study Time for Each Class

Lecture length	Frequency per week	The total hours spent studying per week
1 hour	4 days	8 to 12 hours
3 hours	2 days	12 to 18 hours

As finals approach, you will feel more confident with the subject matter even if the final exam is difficult.

Now you try it:

Course	Lecture length	Frequency per week	Total hours spent studying per week
Total hours per week needed for studying			[Sum of the cells in this column]

HELPFUL HINT

Some exams require more than one or two weeks of studying, such as graduate school entrance exams, board exams, or final exams, when an entire semester is covered. Ask older successful students, graduates, or the professor what they recommend, or check the study guide.

Prioritize the exams and papers that are most important. This can vary by total grade percentage, by points, or by importance, and by due dates or urgency. If everything is important, focus on the subject that presents the greatest challenge.

STUDY THE LEAST FAVORITE SUBJECT FIRST

Study the most challenging or uninteresting subject first. Once we get over an unpleasant task, we feel relieved and motivated. Students might also perform better than expected. If all else fails, recalling how it felt to take the most recent exam, the complexity of emotions about not understating the questions or feeling unprepared, is motivating in itself.

For a subject we don't especially like, we can find alternative ways to understand it or make it relatable to our daily activities. For instance, what might anthropology (one of my least favorite courses) tell us about fraternity life? Not a fan of accounting? Try to apply the principles to streamline your household budget.

When I took organic chemistry, I struggled to make sense of all the electrons—each electron was represented with a dot. To make it easier on myself, I switched the dots to x's and y's, because I enjoyed math so much that I felt I could relate to x's and y's more easily.

Highlighting is not the same as note-taking (which we already covered). The best way to highlight is NOT to start by highlighting. (I consider it one of the biggest mistakes that students make and that I made in my early college years). Instead, we might pick up a highlighter on our *second* pass through the text.

The goal of highlighting is to create a filtering system for two reasons. First, when the exam is close, we will only have time to revisit critical areas or key concepts. Second, if we revisit the material after a year for a cumulative exam, the lack of a filter would mean juggling even more information. In both cases, time is a constraint, so it's best to have a general idea of what areas to focus on first rather than highlighting everything.

MY FOOLPROOF THREE-TIER FILTERING SYSTEM

On the first pass through the material, read everything. Underline or circle essential words or key concepts with a pen or pencil while reading (a pen is ideal for PowerPoints, packets, and handouts, and a pencil for textbooks). If the whole paragraph is important, bracket it (summary paragraphs might fall under this category).

On the second pass, reread everything, focusing more on the underlined areas. If those areas are still necessary or important, highlight them in YELLOW.

On the third pass, read only the YELLOW highlighted areas. If the YELLOW highlighted areas still seem important, re-highlight them in ORANGE, RED, GREEN, or another color that stands out in a sea of yellow.

How do we use this process to study? On the day before the exam and the day of the exam, focus on the ORANGE highlighted areas (usually about one fifth of the text). On cumulative exams, we'll also know exactly where to focus.

Example

Michael Jeffrey Jordan was born on February 17, 1963, in Brooklyn, New York. [1-3] Later his family moved to Wilmington, North Carolina. [1-3] Jordan attended Emsley A. Laney High School in Wilmington, North Carolina, and later attended the University of North Carolina at Chapel Hill, where he received a bachelor's degree in geography. [1-3] Michael Jordan is known worldwide as one of the best basketball players. [1-3]

1. https://www.britannica.com/biography/Michael-Jordan
2. https://www.espn.com/espn/story/_/id/29180943/school-cool-notable-ath-letes-returned-their-college-degrees
3. https://www.sportsrec.com/7568006/a-biography-of-michael-jordan-as-a-high-school-basketball-player

First pass: Read everything and underline the vital information.

Michael Jeffrey Jordan was born on February 17, 1963, in Brooklyn, New York. [1-3] Later his family moved to Wilmington, North Carolina. [1-3] Jordan attended Emsley A. Laney High School in Wilmington, North Carolina, and later attended the University of North Carolina at Chapel Hill, where he received a bachelor's degree in geography. [1-3] Michael Jordan is known worldwide as one of the best basketball players. [1-3]

Second pass: Reread EVERYTHING, focusing on the underlined areas. If those areas still seem necessary, highlight them in YELLOW.

Michael Jeffrey Jordan was born on February 17, 1963, in Brooklyn, New York. [1-3] Later his family moved to Wilmington, North Carolina. [1-3] Jordan attended Emsley A. Laney High School in Wilmington, North Carolina, and later attended the University of North Carolina at Chapel Hill, where he received a bachelor's degree in geography. [1-3] Michael Jordan is known worldwide as one of the best basketball players. [1-3]

Third pass: Read the YELLOW highlighted areas, and if the YELLOW highlighted areas are still essential, re-highlight them in ORANGE or RED.

Michael Jeffrey Jordan was born on February 17, 1963, in Brooklyn, New York. [1-3] Later his family moved to Wilmington, North Carolina. [1-3] Jordan attended Emsley A. Laney High School in Wilmington, North Carolina, and later attended the University of North Carolina at Chapel Hill, where he received a bachelor's degree in geography. [1-3] Michael Jordan is known worldwide as one of the best basketball players. [1-3]

> REPETITION IS THE KEY TO RETENTION.

HELPFUL HINT

It's not always necessary to do three passes through a text. We might understand and memorize everything on our first pass, and there will be times when it might take *more* than three passes to grasp the material. It's dependent on the material and the student.

Shortly after taking the first exam in General Chemistry, I stopped by the professor's office to take a look at the mistakes I had made. Although I performed well, I felt that I could have done better. I also felt so overwhelmed with the material, that approaching the professor was the right thing to do.

After a brief discussion about some exam questions, we moved to what I did to prepare for the exam, especially reading the textbook. I showed her how I had highlighted my text, and she asked if I had picked up a highlighter on my first pass through the material. I had. That's when she told me it's best to start highlighting *after* going through the material at least once; everything looks or feels important through the first pass, because everything is new to us.

Later on, I took some very challenging courses and added the third tier of highlighting, because of time constraints during finals weeks. This was a strategy I applied again and again in graduate school as well.

FLASHCARD USE

As I've mentioned, flashcards are a great tool to keep in your backpack. Why are flashcards so great?

- ▶ They help with reviewing and reinforcing information.

- ▶ They help with avoiding the illusion of knowing all the material.

- ▶ They help with recalling rather than simply recognizing the information.

The key to using flashcards is repetition. The most basic flashcard setup is question-answer, but they can be used for diagrams, pictures, speeches, and anything else we can think of. There are two types of flashcards—paper, and computer/digital flashcards—each with advantages and disadvantages.

PAPER FLASHCARD ADVANTAGES	COMPUTER/DIGITAL FLASHCARD ADVANTAGES
• We can edit in ways the computer won't allow. • We don't need to have an electronic device. • The website might crash or go through maintenance. • We can quickly jump between cards.	• We get through more flashcards in less time. • The graphics are amazing. • Mobility: We can access them from any digital device.

A common question that students ask is, "When do I study my flashcards?" The answer varies based on the subject, but from personal experience, flashcards should be reviewed before rereading the text or notes for the second time. Flashcards shorten the time it takes our brains to memorize and make connections, thereby giving us a more significant benefit when rereading our notes or the book.

Take a moment to practice making paper flashcards.

Step 1: Start with plain paper or notecards, so that you don't waste money on lined or colored paper. We want a background that doesn't feel 'crowded,' where we can quickly write with any colored pen, pencil, or highlighter, and easily read it.

Step 2: Use a pen (black or blue pen) to write the information. To make something to stand out, use a highlighter or underline it with a different color pen.

Step 3: Label the flashcards with a sign, symbol, letter, or number to trace their source (lecture, text, website, etc.).

Examples:

E1 = Exam 1 flashcards

PPT 1 = PowerPoint One flashcards

C1p232 = Chapter 1, page 232

M = Music class

Whether digital or paper, limit the amount of information on the flashcards for speed and efficiency.

> **Too wordy**: Who was the first President of the United States of America?
>
> **More concise**: First U.S. President

Too wordy: The first President of the United States of America is George Washington

More concise: George Washington

The following is a sample of a completed flashcard:

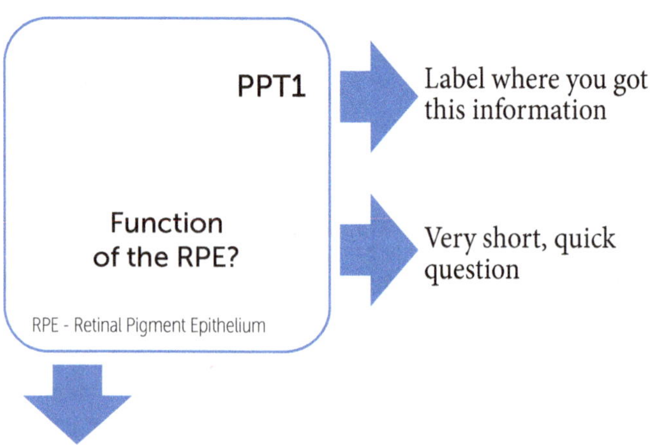

Additional flashcard suggestions:

- Double-check their accuracy.
- Studying flashcards from both sides helps create more neural connections.
- In the last few days before the exam, separate the flashcards into two groups:
    - What I know: The bulk of the flashcards should be here, perhaps 80%.

> ► What I don't know: Less than 20% of the
> cards should be here; if not, have a la-
> ser focus on this material!

My flashcards made the most significant difference in my grades. If I was borderline "B-," then the notecards got me to a solid "B+." I think it's a great tool, probably one of the best tools that students have. My advice is to not wait until classes become extremely challenging before using them.

LEARN THE DETAILS

The most challenging professors are those looking to see if students know the details, not just the 'general concept.' Details can be hard to grasp, especially when learning something new; initially, everything seems important. Here are a few things to look out for:

> ► Understand the general concept to start; af-
> ter you feel comfortable with the gen-
> eral idea, zoom in on the detail.

- ▶ Focus on the information in the small boxes, side notes, referenced images, and so on.
- ▶ Pay attention to the formatting, including symbols, ital-
  ics, bolded words, underlined words, and numbers. In
  some ways, the author has done the work for the reader.

THINK OUTSIDE THE BOX

Professors teaching the same subject for years refine their presentations, adding new findings and trends only when they are impactful. To expand on that knowledge or get a different point of view:

- ▶ Search for online lectures with similar themes, topics, and so on.
- ▶ Find books on the topic by visiting the
  school or community library.
- ▶ Ask the current and other professors who have taught
  or still teach the course to provide additional material.
- ▶ Ask students who took the course for suggestions about sources they found most helpful.

VISUALIZE

Before reading a textbook, packet, or notes, find a video online on the topic (if the notes or packet provided are without visual components); it will help you to visualize what the author conveys in the text. If authors are wordy, visuals will make it easier to grasp the material. For example, if the author describes the heart anatomy, wouldn't it be helpful to study a *diagram or model* of the heart?

GIVE IT TIME

They say hindsight is 20/20, and a difficult concept might take many years to develop. Just as it took time to develop the idea, it takes time to understand it. Thus, repetition and revisiting complex topics is essential.

SAVE IMPORTANT DOCUMENTS

So that students can revisit notes, projects, and papers, a system is needed to organize and store documents. I would highly encourage using plastic storage bins (for physical stuff) and the Cloud system (for digital material) (see the chapter on Materials and Tools for more information).

I recently went out for dinner with an old friend. He wants to return to school and perhaps get a master's degree in psychology, but he got rid of his undergraduate materials when he moved. Although I threw out most of my undergraduate material, I kept my graduate school material. If I ever need a refresher on eye disease, for instance, I only need to open my notes.

TURN IN ASSIGNMENTS EARLY

Form a pattern of finishing and turning in assignments early, or at least of completing the work before the due date. This reduces worry. Professors are also more inclined to forgive students with an excellent track record if they miss a due date than student who are habitually late when submitting work.

PRACTICE AT THE EDGE OF YOUR ABILITY

Push yourself. Just because the exam has only 25 multiple-choice questions doesn't signal you should relax and not worry about it. Instead, pushing yourself beyond the minimum will help prepare for just about anything.

Think of studying like practicing a sport. All athletes practice hard, so that game days are the 'easy' days. Likewise, think of making exam day 'easy.'

MY EXPERIENCE

In graduate school, many different professors taught Diagnosis of Accommodation & Binocular Dysfunction course, because they were all experts on particular subtopics. Before our first exam, we had a couple of easy quizzes, so many classmates decided not to study as hard for our first real exam. Because the exam was short, we all thought, "How bad could it be?" Late in the weekend before the exam, while many classmates hit the bar, I told myself that I was probably over-studying as I decided to stay in versus going out.

The exam was highly challenging, with many different professors writing many different question styles. I did better than most, but not great (by "better," I mean that I earned a high "C"). As you can imagine, many classmates struggled, and no one in the class got an "A." Although a short exam, it was very tough. I never again second-guessed how much studying I thought I needed to prepare for exams.

CHANGE THE STUDY PATTERN

After covering all class notes, consider mixing them up and studying without a pattern or outline, for a different angle on the material. Ask "What if?" questions while moving through the material to make it more exciting and challenging. For example, the book might only discuss bones in the right hand; test yourself on the bones in the left hand as well. Apply the same idea to math, coding, history, and other subjects, then use your core study processes to check your knowledge retention.

ASSESS YOUR STRENGTHS AND WEAKNESSES

As students, we might forget that we don't know everything, that we lack some knowledge, experience, and know-how. Be honest and figure out what you're good at and where you need help. For example, I enjoy history. If I had to read or watch a historical documentary and be quizzed on the subject matter, I would have an easier time than some. Ask family, peers, and professors for their observations. Of course, it can be tough to accept that we are not perfect, but criticism opens the door for improvement and growth.

When offering critical feedback to a close friend, peer, or family member, be honest, precise, factual, and objective. It's best done in private as well.

ONLINE CHAT GROUPS

Online chat groups are communities that share common interests such as art, music, robotics, and other hobbies. Please take advantage of these groups. They are often passionate about helping others. Whether students are posting a question or seeking a reference, someone is usually willing to help.

As with everything we post online, be diligent about not sharing personal information (birth date, full name, phone number, Social Security number, or email address) and not befriending strangers.

In my first semester in college, I would wait until the last minute to do my chemistry homework. As it turned out, sometimes the assignments were more complicated than I had expected, and because I wasn't close to anyone else in class, I relied on the internet for support. When you are out of options, creativity flourishes, and I assumed there must be people who enjoy common subjects. I searched for chemistry forums or chemistry chat groups and quickly found one where I could post questions about my homework and ways to approach the problems. Many people helped, and I got my homework done on time.

Study apps are a great tool when you're on the go and don't have direct access to school's material. There are apps for flashcards, lectures, practice questions, and other tools. Do a little research and figure out what is the best for you (search all the popular study apps, or maybe read up on a forum about them, or ask classmates which apps they use). Some of my favorite apps and other digital tools were Quizlet, YouTube, and Grammarly.

Many websites can aid with studying. I don't endorse any of these; however, the three that helped me were Khan Academy, YouTube, and Quizlet. When stuck on a topic, consider going online and searching the subject on the web. The information is out there; just be sure the sources are reputable and well-established to avoid misinformation. Coming up empty handed? Consider searching for related keywords and issues. So, for example, if nothing pops up on "Illyrians," one might try searching for Thracians, Dacians, Romans, etc. Also consider asking a research librarian for suggestions.

Wikipedia, a free online encyclopedia, is edited by volunteers from across the globe. Although this is not considered a scholarly source—in other words, the material is not submitted to credentialed boards of review, and it is not always fact-checked—*some* of the volunteer editors and writers are very knowledgeable. However, readers can't assume they didn't put their own spin on specific topics. That said, **always double- and triple-check the sources and information from that website**. And from personal experience in an age of misinformation, always double-check and triple-check *everything* you read online.

HAVE SELF-DISCIPLINE

Mother Teresa once said, "Discipline is the bridge between goals and accomplishment." In medicine especially, if something fails, don't blame others. Think of it this way: If a surgery goes wrong, do you think the patient blames the equipment, the staff, or the doctor? Most likely, as the person in charge of treatment, the doctor would take the blame. That is why doctors need to be on-point and disciplined, no matter what. Approach your studies this way and take responsibility for your grades.

MY EXPERIENCE

A fear of failing college was probably my most significant driving factor, yet during my second-to-last semester (in undergrad), I did poorly on an exam. I had studied hard and could not bear the thought that I had received a bad grade. When I went to bed that night, awake and staring at the ceiling, I thought, "Did I give 100% to this class?" (I had found time to waste online and catch up on TV.) That's when it hit me: my self-discipline wasn't even close to what it should have been.

High-level science courses require high-level self-discipline. I realized that the more advanced the courses I took, the harder they would become, so using the same tactics wouldn't produce success. My discipline then became so extreme that semester that I don't think I even relaxed until my second year in graduate school!

DO WELL EARLY IN THE SEMESTER

I'll end this chapter back at the beginning: the better a student does early in the semester, the less stress they will have later in the school year. In addition, exams tend to become more challenging as the school year progresses (the material builds on itself). By doing better early on, students have a cushion to rely on. Even after a low grade on a project, paper, proficiency, and so on, there is enough wiggle room to recover by the end of the course. If you do not do well early in the semester, I strongly encourage you to approach the professor and discuss your situation with them. It's better to talk to your professor throughout the semester rather than wait until the end of the semester.

CHAPTER 8

LAST-MINUTE TECHNIQUES

"Procrastination? No, I just wait until the last minute
to do my work because I will be older, therefore wiser."
~ Will Ferrell, in Anchorman

Although this quote is meant to bring a chuckle, the reality is that there won't always be enough time to study all the material for an exam. Whatever the reason (procrastination, schedules, health issues), it will happen at some point. This chapter addresses that reality. The following study suggestions are valuable, so don't use them only for last-minute cramming.

DON'T PANIC

Easier said than done, but when bracing for a last-minute exam, best not to panic but to focus and tune into what *can* be done with limited time. If you are still not confident enough with the material, accept it as a normal feeling. Start by being very realistic about the grade you might earn, with the primary goal of *passing the test*.

Research conducted at Stanford University found that multitasking is less productive than doing a single thing at a time.[2] The researchers also found that people who are regularly bombarded with several streams of electronic information cannot pay attention, recall information, or switch from one job to another as well as those who complete one task at a time. Think of multitasking as driving on a busy freeway, but while on the phone, eating food, and listening to music. Concentration will be lost, as will the ability to absorb information.

MY EXPERIENCE

While an undergrad, the school library was one of my favorite places to study. Four stories tall, each floor served a specific purpose, where the first and second floors were reserved for group studying and the third and fourth floors were reserved for quiet study. Although I might have intended to learn on the second floor, I also wanted to socialize. Unfortunately, although this study spot worked for some exams, it did not work for all of them, and I learned a fundamental lesson. If I was genuinely going to study, I needed 100% dedication without any distractions. I couldn't expect great results if I didn't put my best foot forward.

---

2 https://www.forbes.com/sites/travisbradberry/2014/10/08/multitasking-damages-your-brain-and-career-new-studies-suggest/?sh=770ae48e56ee

ADDRESS A PROBLEM ON YOUR OWN

Initially, try to approach any problem alone in order to think critically. If our friend solves the problem, it gives a false sense of security and leads to the assumption that we understand the material. Approaching the problem alone provides an idea of what we don't yet understand.

MY EXPERIENCE

I love chess. It's a very strategic game, and at first, I would watch others play, assuming that if I copied their moves, I would know how to play better. This wasn't the case. I had a false sense of confidence and did not do well when applying similar moves. In school, we can create our own strategies first and then ask for advice or guidance.

DON'T SKIP UNFAMILIAR TERMS

When was the last time you saw an eye doctor? Was it an optometrist or an ophthalmologist? In general, if you need glasses or contact lenses, you are more likely to see an optometrist, but if you need eye surgery, you are more likely to see an ophthalmologist. Unfortunately, such terms get mixed up by many people—including students. If you read a textbook or even a PowerPoint presentation and don't understand a specific term, don't mix-and-match. Instead, take a moment to look up the definition or ask the instructor for clarification.

Every PowerPoint presentation or book generally follows a pattern. As we saw in our discussion of note-taking, flowcharts break down the pattern into simple ideas we can easily understand, much like a road map sketches our route. Make a flow chart like this one, to simplify complex concepts, to understand the logic of the presented material, and to debug possible exam questions:

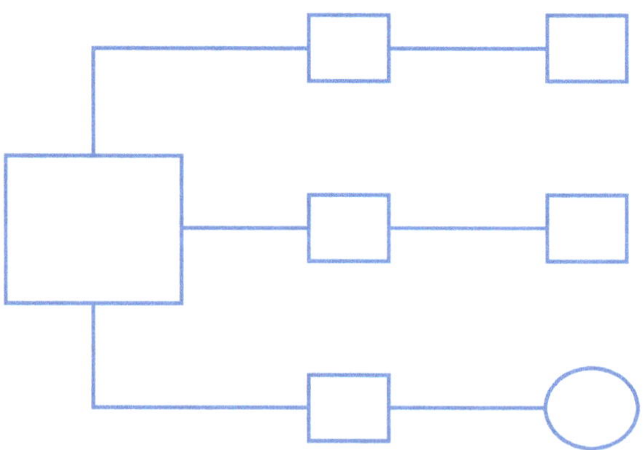

Tables are an easy tool to create and are helpful in organizing information and thoughts, especially when:

- ▶ Comparing multiple items (e.g., memorizing differences and similarities between different bacteria)
- ▶ Comparing book characters
- ▶ Learning a foreign language (such as listing grammar or verb tenses)
- ▶ Comparing diseases
- ▶ Comparing data values

Many resources are available online to help better understand how to use tables and graphics to present data. Try a search to see what works for you!

MY EXPERIENCE

Because French is a highly complex language, one of my high school teachers said that if we wanted to learn a word and have it engrained forever, we needed to write it 25 times. To save time with writing, I would type it into a table, along with verb tenses. The tables made it easy to jump from cell to cell, and I never got tired of typing.

Acronyms are handy when trying to remember a large amount of information. Some popular acronyms that we use daily are:

- ASAP (as soon as possible)
- PIN (personal identification number)
- GIF (graphics interchange format)

Be creative by forming acronyms while studying. It's a fun and effective memory tool.

MY EXPERIENCE

In graduate school, we took multiple pharmacology classes and learned about many medications. It was essential to figure out ways to remember them. Some of my favorite acronyms are listed in this table:

MALE:	**RIPE:**
▶ Macugen ▶ Avastin ▶ Lucentis ▶ Eylea **USED TO TREAT MACULAR DEGENERATION.**	▶ Rifamycin ▶ Isoniazid ▶ Pyrazinamide ▶ Ethambutol **USED TO TREAT TUBERCULOSIS.**

ON YOUR JOURNEY TO SUCCESS

List the acronyms you like to use:

MNEMONICS

Mnemonics create associations that assist in remembering something. Mnemonics are great if you can find a direct link between what you are learning and something familiar. For example, I first named this book *The Art of Studying* and used the Italian flag's three colors for the word "Art" (since Italy is known for its art). A common mnemonic used in math is, "Please Excuse My Dear Aunt Sally," which stands for Parentheses, Exponent, Multiplication, Division, Addition, and Subtraction. (So, when you do a math problem, you first do whatever is in parentheses, then apply exponents, and so forth.) This is a great tool to group large chunks of information; use it often.

CUT YOUR LOSSES

Imagine it's the night before the exam; a student is stuck trying to decipher a topic she hasn't understood over the past few weeks. She has two options: spend the rest of the night trying to understand this complex topic or use her time to review the rest of her notes. At this point, I would recommend that she cut her losses and focus on the bulk of the material, not the concept that still escapes her.

Similarly, if we take a multiple-choice exam and get stuck on one question, we can ask, "Should I spend more time with this question, or skip it and make an educated guess?" Consider the point value, and if it's not worth the time, move on.

***

Congratulations on completing Part II! Pat yourself on the back and take time to unwind before moving to the final part of the book!

PART III

STUDENT LIFE

CHAPTER 9

TAKING EXAMS

"Push yourself, because no one else
is going to do it for you."
~ Unknown

Examinations and tests are a staple of one's college education. All the studying and all the preparation come down to taking an exam. For some students, exams are just another hoop that they have to jump through; for others, it's a terrifying experience that they have to go through. This chapter, then, is dedicated not to study tips, but to the *process* of taking an examination.

In my opinion, the more exams a student takes, the more confidence they will build, regardless of what is being tested or the length of the exam. With time students can learn how to handle stress, dive into the exam, and, most importantly, be successful; however, don't automatically assume success from the start. Test-taking might be a skill to improve over time; practice and repetition make perfect.

DON'T LET EVERYONE KNOW ABOUT YOUR BIG DAY

Besides your inner circle of friends and immediate family, I would avoid sharing the exam day with anyone else. Why? The exam could be easy, or it could be a nightmare in the making; do we want everyone to know about it? The conversation might lead to the burden of questions about whether we are ready, or if we think will pass, and so on. Not sharing means one less thing to worry about.

MY EXPERIENCE

I needed to take the Optometry Admission Test (OAT) to apply to an optometry program. Because many of my peers knew that I needed to take the exam, I was often asked if I had taken it yet. By this point, I knew better than to say "yes" right away, because I knew the follow-up question would be, "How did you do?" Causing unnecessary anxiety. Not sharing too much information turned out to be a pearl of wisdom.

As you prepare for an exam, ask the instructor about the exam setup, because it might differ depending on the teacher. Some questions to ask are:

- ▶ Is there a study guide for the exam?
- ▶ Is it a multiple-choice exam, free response, or both?
- ▶ What is the exam date(s)?
- ▶ How much time is allowed?
- ▶ Will this exam be about as difficult or more demanding than those taken so far?
- ▶ How well do students generally do, and what do they struggle with?
- ▶ Is there a possibility to retake it?
- ▶ Is there an opportunity for extra credit?

It helps to focus one's studying based on the instructor's answers.

Expect the unexpected. To prevent cheating, professors might switch the standard exam format. Also, if most exams have been relatively easy so far, consider preparing to take a challenging exam next time.

MY EXPERIENCE

In my college career, only a handful of professors kept the same question pattern in their exams. In those cases, each exam was weighted the same toward our grades, and students always knew what to expect. The other professors, though, varied their exams about mid-semester, often presenting a very tough exam, many different types of questions, or a new exam setup.

PRACTICE USING OLD EXAMS

Some professors provide old exams, so that students can familiarize themselves with how the questions are worded. If old exams are not provided, see if the textbook offers practice quizzes or if you can find online exams that cover similar topics. The textbook publisher might also provide practice tests.

MOCK TESTS

Taking mock tests helps students to overcome text anxiety and feel ready for an exam. Ideally, to build a mock test, make the questions harder than anticipated, in order to practice at the edge of one's ability. Time the mock test as the instructor would, perhaps even taking it at the same time of day or in the same lecture hall.

Mock tests can take time to create. If you have time, and feel it's necessary to reduce test anxiety, partner with a few classmates and build one together.

Before picking up the notes to study, scan the entire study guide and its table of contents. This only takes a few minutes, but helps direct your focus, as we might tend to overlook specific topics, especially during a time crunch. If a study guide is not provided, create one, or ask classmates if they have already made one.

While study guides can be beneficial, they don't necessarily cover everything. I would often rely solely on my notes, assuming that all lecture information might be on the exam.

GROUP STUDY

For major exams, group studying usually occurs a few days prior. Group studying helps test students' knowledge of the material and allows them to better understand the subject.

How to prepare for a group study or review session:

- ▶ Form a group of three to five classmates (larger groups are inefficient). Friends don't necessarily have to be part of this group; it is better to have only classmates who seem to take the subject seriously.

- ▶ Show up prepared and ready to go, not still waking up and looking for coffee!

- ▶ Bring all course materials and your questions.

- ▶ Have a format and agenda for what the group will cover.

- ▶ Ideally, set aside between one and three hours for a session.

- ▶ Consider having short breaks to use the restroom, check messages, or take a quick walk outside to keep energized.

- ▶ Pick a meeting place that works for everyone.

- ▶ If possible, reserve a group study room or a conference room that's private and quiet enough so that everyone can hear. (Remember to reserve the study rooms early, because midterm and finals times can make them scarce.)

- ▶ Consider a Zoom study group if you can't meet in person.

- ▶ Put away and turn off all cell phones while reviewing!

For introverts or others who like to study alone, consider some of these advantages of studying with others:

- Group studying helps build or fine-tune interpersonal skills.
- Peers can motivate each other to study harder.
- Learning is more fun when jokes and stories are shared.
- Classmates might encourage each other to think differently.

REMEMBER TO RESERVE STUDY ROOMS EARLY BECAUSE MIDTERM AND FINALS TIMES CAN MAKE STUDY ROOMS SCARCE.

HELPFUL HINTS

- Studying and reviewing in a group *during exam day* can cause anxiety, so schedule this activity ahead of the exam.
- Studying with someone you know is behind in their studies might not help; be wise about choosing group members.

SURVEYS

Surveys are a great instrument to use with your classmates and even professors. They serve a multitude of purposes. Here are just a few examples of when to use surveys:

- ▶ Requesting a different exam date
- ▶ Making decisions in group projects
- ▶ Stimulating discussions
- ▶ Debating a point about a subject or topic
- ▶ Having a baseline from which to compare results over time

Finally, proceed with caution. Like any tool, surveys should be used—not overused—when needed. Unless the professor is teaching survey design, every moment spent designing, distributing, and reviewing surveys is time subtracted from lectures and studying. The clock is ticking, so be sure the issue is worth the time and effort.

USE SURVEYS WITH CAUTION AND BE SURE THE ISSUE IS WORTH THE (POSSIBLY) HEATED DEBATE AS WELL AS THE TIME AND EFFORT.

Success while taking an exam means not being tired, overworked, or emotionally distracted. Plan the day around the exam. Wake up an hour earlier than usual and review the most important concepts to keep yourself on track and focused.

- ▶ I suggest not spending more than an hour reviewing the material, because it can lead to feeling burned out.

- ▶ Waking up too early could also be a problem if the exam is in the evening.

- ▶ If more than two exams are scheduled in one day, consider asking the professors if you can take one on a different date.

There is a saying that goes, "Early is on time, on time is late, and late is unacceptable!" Arriving early allows time to calm down and mentally prepare rather than rushing to get to the exam. Consider waiting in your car or the library if the classroom environment arouses anxiety. If commuting, consider leaving home 30 minutes to an hour early, in case of unexpected traffic. (Rather than give some students less time than others, some professors will not allow students to take exams if they arrive after the scheduled start time.)

TAKE CARE OF BASIC NEEDS

Be 100% focused on the exam during the big day and not distracted by basic needs. For example, before the exam, use the restroom, drink (or pack) water, maybe eat a small snack, and bring tissues for a runny nose (which are probably already in your well-stocked backpack!).

DURING THE EXAM

When first receiving the exam, consider doing a brain dump (writing formulas, acronyms, and key facts) on the exam paper, especially if you're worried about forgetting something. As a second step, write your name immediately, if the exam is provided on paper. Finally, quickly skim the entire exam, looking at the number of questions, the format (multiple-choice, free-response, a mixture of the two, or essays). Each student is different; however, I suggest answering the free-response questions first. Then, address multiple choice or true/false questions, if needed; when time is short, you can always guess.

Next, read the instructions carefully and underline or circle any keywords. Answer and respond to as many questions as possible, without focusing on one question for any extended period. You can skip around between questions, answering the easy ones first. Make sure, though, to mark the questions skipped, as a reminder to revisit them later.

A rule of thumb: I found that the more questions I skipped or put reminders for myself to revisit, the worse I did on the exam. If I skipped ten questions, I automatically assumed that at least half of those responses would be incorrect. Skipping questions also leads to our next topic.

MIND THE CLOCK

Keep track of time, whether by watching the clock or listening for the instructor's prompts. I would also encourage you to write down the start time *before* the exam; that way, you know exactly how many minutes you have left—every second counts. Some professors allow extra time; others don't and tend to clarify that on the first day of the semester. If professors allow students to stay later, be respectful of their time, because they have other classes to teach.

DOUBLE-CHECK

After completing the exam, take some time to double-check the answers before you hand in the exam (time permitting).

HELPFUL HINT

Some might argue that it's wrong to double-check your answers, because we often second-guessing ourselves; however, I think that if you know the material well, that won't happen. And you might catch some errors. Consider: when you lock the door, do you ever check to make sure it's closed?

ASK FOR CLARIFICATION

When taking the exam, some questions or words might seem ambiguous. New professors, for example, might still be testing the waters and haven't perfected their technique. If so, always ask for clarification. And if unsure about the test-taking directions, ask the professor.

For efficiency, either raise your hand or group all questions and ask them at the very end of the time allotted. While some classmates might find this distracting, others might thank you for asking for clarification (if they are too shy to approach the professor). In any case, try to keep your voice low when others are concentrating.

AFTER THE EXAM

When feeling anxious after an exam, I found it was best to avoid talking to anyone afterward and to take time to relax instead. Learning from classmates that one got a question wrong, for instance, could cause needless stress and worry, especially if grades aren't posted immediately.

MY EXPERIENCE

After finishing a big exam, I would go home to sleep, relax, and watch TV. Nothing irritated me more than talking to my classmates about the exam. If someone asked about it, I would tell them, "Hey, it's over. Let's talk about something else," or I would try to change the subject. By that point, I needed to clear my head!

CHECK EXAM RESULTS

After grades are released, ask your professor if you can review the exam. Unless you got 100% and didn't struggle with anything, the mistakes, or even challenging questions, might show up on the final or in a different class.

HELPFUL HINT

If every question on the exam seems ambiguous or challenging and/or your exam grade seems much lower than usual, discuss it with the professor after the exam. Perhaps others had difficulties with the questions as well.

Whether going to a nice restaurant or going out with friends, rewarding yourself after spending weeks studying is a **good idea**. It gives you something to look forward to, and it might even motivate you to work harder on the next exam.

ON YOUR JOURNEY TO SUCCESS

Use this space to list the activities, places, or other low-cost rewards you might enjoy after the next big exam:

I loved taking exams on Friday and if I knew I did well, I could go out and celebrate stress-free. Monday exams were less fun. Especially in a Detroit winter, there wasn't much to do on Monday night!

MANAGE YOUR EMOTIONS

This doesn't mean letting emotions control us. Think instead of feelings as having a domino effect. When we get frustrated with an exam we cannot focus on other essential tasks and decisions. As a result, we are more likely to make other mistakes. And that creates more stress. On the other hand, when we do well, we might get too confident and comfortable, which increases the likelihood of a mistake. Whether the grade was excellent or poor, acknowledge and manage your emotions to avoid these extremes.

MY EXPERIENCE

I would often feel emotional after doing poorly on an exam, especially in graduate school, because I had worked hard and had nothing to show for it. Still, I learned how to manage these feelings by doing two things: praying and working out. I started going to church more and would also try to run or walk more often. These two very different activities allowed me to collect my thoughts and my strength to do better going forward.

I hope this chapter helps readers to stay calm on test day. If anxiety persists, please consider additional resources, professional support, or these books:

Unwinding Anxiety: New Science Show How to Break the Cycles of Worry and Fear to Heal Your Mind, by Judson Brewer, MD, PhD

Rewire Your Anxious Brain: How to Use the Neuroscience of Fear to End Anxiety, Panic, and Worry by Catherine M. Pittman PhD and Elizabeth M. Karle, MLIS

CHAPTER 10

NETWORKING

"It's not who you know—it's who knows you!"
~ David Avrin

Learning how to create new relationships, cultivate old relationships, and expand our network will serve us well in education and in professional life. Genuine relationships lead to personal growth in areas such as emotional health, motivation, and social intelligence. As we end a college career, we need to keep this in mind, because while school ends, professional relationships are only just beginning.

BUILDING RELATIONSHIPS WITH PROFESSORS

Strong professional relationships with instructors are essential, especially in the early college years. The benefits of having a solid professional relationship include that potential future reference or letter of recommendation, but it doesn't have to be limited to those concerns. Professional relationships could lead to becoming a tutor for the course or a teaching assistant.

A trusted professor can be a compass in helping to guide students in their academic and professional life. As students continue their college journeys, they might decide to teach one day. The same professor with whom they developed an authentic relationship might offer support or guidance. Consider introducing yourself to the professor, no matter how large the lecture or class. It only takes a moment but can have lasting benefits.

For relationship building during online courses, consider contacting the professor or instructor via email and introducing yourself. Make time to meet during their virtual office hours. I would also try to meet in person unless the school is too far away. Finally, I strongly encourage participation in class forums or discussion boards.

ON YOUR JOURNEY TO SUCCESS

Reflect on teachers or other mentors you've known over the years, either in or outside of school. Where and how did you meet them? What was most helpful about that interaction? What knowledge or skills did you gain? Now ask yourself, "What knowledge or skills do I need *today*? Who has those skills or that expertise and might be a good mentor?"

Although I am now in my early career, I still try to stop by and visit some of my old professors when I get a chance. Some have retired since I finished college, but I still try to say 'hello'. I enjoy touring the colleges and lecture halls to reminisce and reflect on my professional growth.

MAKE FRIENDS

Build strong bridges that last a lifetime. Friends will boost students' happiness and may lead to more opportunities as well. It helps to get different perspectives and viewpoints, too, whether on schoolwork or life lessons. One day, one of those friendships might carry over into your work life, whether as a business partner or a job contact.

HELPFUL HINT

If you try to be everyone's best friend, you will likely never have enough time for yourself or your family. Some friendships might become superficial. You can't be best friends with everybody, but you can *respect* them. It's good practice for networking as well.

GET INVOLVED

I encourage students to join a few social or professional organizations or at least to attend their meetings. Being involved in these activities will help develop interpersonal, team-building, and leadership skills. Joining a new organization also teaches different perspectives and viewpoints. Experiencing something new and stepping out of our comfort zones also makes us well-rounded people. For example, a potluck might offer delicious new foods as well as a chance to learn more about other cultures and meet new people.

MY EXPERIENCE

The University of Michigan-Dearborn and Wayne State University have a diverse student body, so I made friends from all over the world, from Nigeria to Poland to Thailand. Because of my experiences, I learned much more about different cultures. Today, in my practice, I can apply that knowledge to better serve the whole community.

TRUST TAKES TIME

I asked my grandpa (now 88 years old) how to tell the difference between a good friend and a bad friend; he said, "Just give it time. Just because someone does you a favor or acts nice does not make them loyal or trustworthy." As the expression goes, "Rome wasn't built in a day." We need time to figure people out and to build trust. More importantly, you need time to figure *yourself* out in the process.

NETWORKING

Formal networking provides a new avenue of opportunities as we finish our education and jump into the workforce. It's crucial to network regularly, through social gatherings, online, or during continuing education. First, start cultivating solid relationships with classmates, professors, and everyone in daily life. Then, just as we benefited from strong relationships, we can make sure we pay it forward by helping others.

Because friends guided me through my early phases of undergrad, I tried doing the same thing for others as I finished undergrad and started graduate school. The students I mentored now work in different fields. Although we were all students at one point, we are now all successful in our respective fields, where the networking and sharing of ideas continue. To this day, we have genuine trust and respect for one another.

ATTEND EVENTS

Limiting oneself to studying can undermine growth potential and perhaps even hold students back in the ever-changing work-life environment. College is the time to experience as many things as we can. Whether listening to guest speakers, going to movie nights, or attending a conference or a fundraiser, these events allow students to meet people and gain knowledge, and to experience something new and different.

If friends invite us to visit another school, we can make the time. If invited to a concert, then attend! In fact, if attending an event makes the difference between a "B+" and a "B," I might take the "B" and attend an event. Why? Because as the years pass, we won't necessarily remember the grades, but we will remember the events and the memories shared with peers.

In brief: there is no substitute for enjoying life. Spending a few hours having fun does not detract from your academic gains.

CHAPTER 11

STAYING HEALTHY

*"A good laugh and a long sleep are the
best cures in the doctor's book."*
~ Irish proverb

It is important to stay healthy as you push your mind and body to their maximum. If you do, you will have great energy, stamina, and mental acuity to apply to your studies. Also, staying fit through college will give you the extra energy to get over any bumps in the road. It's never too late (or too early) to take your health seriously.

MEDICAL AND EYE EXAMS

Consider getting annual checkups. Regular checkups with the family doctor or general practitioner can help catch problems early and lead to healthier lives. Eye exams are essential when we ask our eyes to work daily. A slight adjustment in a lens prescription or some vision therapy might help tremendously, allowing students to study longer with fewer problems.

MY EXPERIENCE

As an eye doctor, I see many patients struggling with their vision around finals time. The main complaint is blurry vision at a distance. This primarily occurs when students spend too much time in front of a screen and don't take enough breaks between studying. Although I do a thorough eye exam, I always bring up the need for study breaks. Similarly, a minor prescription tweak helps, but new glasses are not always the whole solution. If you notice a change in your vision, check in with your optometrist.

NUTRITION

You might have heard the phrase, "You are what you eat." If you eat nutritious food, you will be healthier. Whether studying at the library, school, or at home, keep a bottle of water and a few healthy snacks handy (rather than risk eating empty calories from vending machines).

Other health habits to consider while studying:

- ▶ Drinking enough water to stay hydrated.
- ▶ Not overeating: It can lead to drowsiness, and it's not healthy.
- ▶ Eating breakfast daily! Even if it's a small amount of food, it's still the most important meal of the day.
- ▶ Avoiding too much caffeine or sugary foods.

▶ Planning and cooking meals: It's efficient, cost-saving, and nutritious. Do this once or twice a week.

No one is perfect, but see how many nutrition tips you can implement today.

Using your calendar or planner, record your food intake for one week. Note the times of day as well. The goal is not dieting or weight change, but to become more aware of any obstacles to good nutrition.

My coffee addiction started while working as a barista at age 15. As I got a little older and the responsibilities kept growing, I started to have a cup here and there, and before I knew it, I was addicted! I then needed a cup after school as I did my homework as well. Later, a friend introduced me to so-called energy drinks in college. This caffeine addiction only got worse in graduate school. By then, I realized that I was overdoing it, so to limit my intake, I took steps like switching to tea in the morning and coffee only in the afternoon. I now limit my caffeine intake to a cup of coffee a day.

EXERCISE

Exercise helps us stay healthy, energetic, and motivated. Cardio, weights, swimming, or yoga—anything to get the blood flowing is a plus. No time to work out? Consider adding extra steps to your daily routine by taking the stairs or parking your car farther from the classroom. And the campus probably has its own onsite gym or pool!

> **USE COMMON SENSE, AND ASK YOUR DOCTOR BEFORE STARTING A NEW ROUTINE, FOLLOWING THE GUIDELINES FOR YOUR AGE, WEIGHT, AND ABILITY.**

MY EXPERIENCE

I prefer to go to the community center versus a members-only gym because it tends to be less busy than regular gyms and quieter.

Study breaks help learners to retain the material. They also minimize head-aches, eye strain, boredom, and other obstacles to studying. My recommendation is a 15- to 30-minute break after one hour of learning. Also, get up and stretch often for about one to three minutes for better blood flow and less neck or back pain.

Why do I recommend that you study for one hour, non-stop? Because the length of typical college class without a break is roughly an hour. So essentially, studying becomes training for listening to lectures and taking exams.

In graduate school, I often went grocery shopping or on a coffee run during my breaks. This helped me take my mind off studying but also made my use of time more efficient.

The health benefits of getting enough sleep are enormous, from reducing stress to keeping your heart healthy to making you more alert and improving your memory. In a recent podcast interview with Joe Rogan, Elon Musk (a modern-day inventor and entrepreneur) mentioned that he gets at least six hours of sleep a night, and that his total productivity decreases with less. All that said, don't pull an all-nighter. Instead, especially before a big exam, get at least seven to nine hours of sleep per night, waking up only an hour earlier than usual to review the material.

NAPS

A post on the *Sleepscore* blog titled "How Long Should a Nap Be?" stated:

- 10- to 20-minute naps are also referred to as power naps.[3] These short naps allow you to wake up feeling refreshed, energized, and alert.[3] To sweeten the deal, well-timed power naps have little to no impact on your nighttime slumber, so you can head to sleep at your usual bedtime without any difficulty dozing off.[3]

▶ 90-minute naps allow you to cycle through all sleep stages while avoiding sleep inertia, since you're not waking up during deep sleep.[3] This leaves you feeling thoroughly rejuvenated, more creative, more focused, and more physically energized.[3]

If this is not enough to convince you of the benefits of sleep, did you know that Albert Einstein used to take naps when solving difficult problems?

MY EXPERIENCE

I loved taking naps while in both undergrad and graduate school. I would look forward to them after a long day because they helped clear my mind, so I woke up refreshed and ready to go. Even as a professional, if I've had a demanding day with patients, I try to squeeze in a short nap in the evening.

---

3 https://www.sleepscore.com/blog/how-long-should-i-nap/#:~:text=According%20to%20the%20National%20Sleep,refreshed%2C%20energized%2C%20and%20alert.

TAKE A DAY OFF

Schedule permitting, I recommend we all take a day off from studying at least once a week. It's something to look forward to, and our brains will have a much-needed break, allowing us to work diligently the rest of the week.

MY EXPERIENCE

In my undergrad days, I would always take off Friday nights from school-work. I was burned out from all the coursework throughout the week, and most of my friends would go out then, so it worked in my favor to forget about school for a time and just socialize.

CRISIS RESOURCES

Psychological crises can happen to anyone at any point. Some might even experience thoughts of self-harm. Or a living situation could simply go sour. Perhaps an addiction to or withdrawal from drugs or alcohol is a pressing concern. Even something that others see as a small problem might affect you in a big way.

When in the midst of a crisis, don't fall into the trap of believing that there is no one to help. In reality, schools offer many resources to help students, from counseling centers and support groups to general information and outside agency referrals. Reach out to the larger community off campus and get the support you need. And if you know of a close friend or relative going through a difficult situation, encourage them to use available resources as well.

MY EXPERIENCE

Using crisis resources is a very personal topic, because I lost a friend to suicide during my third year of undergrad. He was one of the most incredible people I've ever met—kind, warm, and full of joy. Whenever we had a problem within student organizations, he was great at resolving issues and de-escalating stressful situations. I was crushed when I received that phone call late in the evening during class. I wish I had known what he was going through or what was bothering him. This taught me that sometimes the people who are always smiling face the most significant life challenges. It never hurts to ask, "How are you doing?"

CHAPTER 12

ALONG THE JOURNEY

*"Luck is when an opportunity comes
along, and you're prepared for it."*
~ Denzel Washington

You've come a long way since Chapter One and will go even farther while in college! Studying and success in school are just as important as paying attention to everything around you. As one's degree program unfolds, the world is also ever-evolving. Every event, no matter how big or small, impacts our lives more than ever, in part because we are always connected virtually.

After the recent pandemic, many businesses reassessed how they would adapt their processes and move forward. It was the same for students, too, transferring from in-person classes to online only. Some embraced the change and adapted to the new technology while others fell behind.

It's wise to take a good look around, because we never know when an opportunity might appear or when a life-changing event might happen. Don't lose track of who you are, where you are, or where you want to go.

It doesn't hurt to dream, but it's better to be prepared. While we've focused intently on success in college, it's also good to have a backup plan(s) in case something doesn't go our way. Having a backup plan—whether for coursework, finances, housing, or our work life—offers some peace of mind, which can help us stay focused and to better calibrate the next move.

MY EXPERIENCE

I started college in fall 2008, while the economy was going through a recession. Therefore, picking the right major was imperative, because I needed to find a field with many job opportunities and room for growth. I was also aware of some of my limitations, and that my dream of becoming an optometrist might not come true. Acknowledging these realities, I had a bag of alternatives in case optometry didn't work out (such as getting an MBA or becoming a lawyer). With a backup plan in place, I was motivated to attend graduate school while staying open to alternatives.

Unlike the long-range goal of earning a college degree or entering a profession, a short-term development goal can be accomplished in six months, one year, or less. Consider, for example:

- Identifying and developing a new skill, such as coding.
- Fostering an artistic talent.
- Learning a new language.
- Reading a new book every week or month, depending on the amount of free time available.

Such goals help to foster personal growth and keep life interesting!

ON YOUR JOURNEY TO SUCCESS

List three developmental goals that you would enjoy reaching during your college years. Adjust the timelines as needed.

1. ______________________________

2. ______________________________

3. ______________________________

My developmental goal in college was becoming confident during interviews. I prepared by learning more about the company (doing my research), by asking friends and family for good potential interview questions, and through practice, practice, practice.

CONSIDER AN INTERNSHIP

Students need hands-on experience even as they go through school. Of course, they need to know the science, but applied knowledge is just as crucial. Many schools offer internship placements so that students can get this opportunity to use their skills. Internships also help to develop individual students in ways that books and exams cannot.

The goal is to get a foot in the door. If internships or training related to a field of study aren't available, volunteering at an organization involved in that field could help. Moreover if a position is vacant in the same organization, the hiring manager might be more inclined to select a volunteer they know versus someone from the outside.

Students often begin by talking with academic counselors. Other options to consider are becoming a teaching assistant (TA) or looking into other on-campus opportunities, such as work-study programs. From these experiences, a different world opens up.

BE A PROFESSIONAL STUDENT

Always respect your professors, the TA, staff, and others involved in the educational process, regardless of their position. Use their preferred title, such as "Sir", "Doctor," or "Professor." Being kind and courteous with everyone will take you far. We never know who is watching or paying attention to our attitude. You never know when you will need a professional reference.

> **YOU NEVER KNOW WHEN YOU WILL NEED A PROFESSIONAL REFERENCE.**

ONLINE PRESENCE AND SOCIAL MEDIA

Most of us have or have had social media accounts. I was 18 when I got my first account, and it didn't seem like a big deal. Yet we live in a world where, for many reasons, we need to be concerned about what we post and perhaps even about things we posted years ago. And more and more colleges and employers are looking at online social media accounts to research job candidates. Although I don't think a single post defines a person, it's easy to see how someone might misinterpret our statements. Be considerate and kind with your posts because it may be used to define you.

Security is another concern. Ways to keep safe from hackers and other strangers include:

- ► Making sure your privacy settings are turned off from public view.

- ► Not befriending strangers.

- ► Being discreet in everything that you post (less is better).

Many websites offer additional tips on how to be more responsible with social media, including:

- ► **https://youthfirstinc.org/using-social-media-responsibly/**

- ► **https://www.cukeragency.com/blog/2020/10/14/10-ways-to-use-social-media-more-responsibly/**

ON YOUR JOURNEY TO SUCCESS

One of the easiest and most important actions for protecting online security is to change passwords regularly. *Pause here to make a list of your social media, financial, and school accounts.* If you haven't updated your passwords in the past six months, do so now. Then make a note in your calendar to update them again next semester.

CONTINUOUSLY UPDATE YOUR RESUME AND CURRICULUM VITAE

Keep your resume and curriculum vitae (CV) updated. A copy will be requested when you apply for a job or a professional program, and you don't want to scramble at the last minute to put something together.

Visit these websites for ideas about building your resume and CV:

<u>Resume</u>

- ► **https://resumegenius.com/**
- ► **https://www.canva.com/create/resumes/**

<u>CV</u>

- ► **https://www.visualcv.com/**
- ► **https://cvmkr.com/**

Building a resume begins in college. For instance, if you can't find an organization to join, demonstrate leadership skills by starting one! (I'll share my own story later in the chapter.) Consider to volunteer in the community or on campus.

Like learning how to learn, learning how to quickly adapt to changing circumstances is important. College courses will change (perhaps we'll have more exams or more time in the classroom), and they will also get more complex as our college years come to an end. How we adapt to work life will determine whether we succeed.

Unlike some others skills, agility and adaptation is transferrable and follows us into the workforce. We've all seen the ups and downs of the economy in the past several years, and how both employers and employees adapt determines whether they continue to have choices and to be successful. Without the ability to adapt, we might even find ourselves stuck in uncomfortable employment situations.

MY EXPERIENCE

During my second semester as an undergraduate, I had a five-hour gap between my morning and evening classes. I decided to drive back home rather than spend that time at school. Unfortunately, going to and from school took about 30 minutes, so I wasted about an hour on that mid-day commute. I did this for a few weeks, until I ran into an older friend who recommended getting involved at school rather than driving back home. Therefore, to make better use of my downtime, I started the first pre-optometry club on campus! You might do something similar, or if studying at home is difficult, the extra time on campus could be a perfect solution.

BELIEVE IN YOURSELF

Ups and downs are part of any education; but, no matter how challenging certain situations may feel, remember that they are also temporary and will pass. Life is meant to be experienced, and we must believe in ourselves, no matter how hard things get.

MY EXPERIENCE

Like everyone else, I have had many ups and downs (broken relationships, health problems, insufficient finances, and deaths in the family). Some were harder than others, and there were times when I felt that these problems were weighing me down. Yet I ultimately realized that this is part of life, and that those experiences were normal. Knowing that, I believed that I could get past the hurdles.

AVOID COMPARING YOURSELF TO OTHERS

I left this suggestion for the very end of the book, because although I have offered my best guidance, you, the reader, are a unique individual with your own strengths and weaknesses.

Perhaps your peers have had many more opportunities. If so, then use that as a motivation to work harder and smarter. On the other hand, you could be among the lucky ones who have had greater privileges and opportunities. If so, use that awareness to be generous toward others who may be struggling and to withhold judgment.

Ultimately, we can each learn to appreciate our *own* successes, and rather than stacking ourselves against others, we can stand with them!

CONCLUSION

Someone who has completed a journey naturally has advice and stories to share. I hope that my experiences and suggestions help you to prosper in anything you do. Also, if you found the study suggestions helpful, offer them to peers, friends, and loved ones who might benefit. (If someone approached me and suggested something to improve my life, I would keep my ears open!) And one day, when you earn your degree and land that dream job, consider sharing your own story!

APPENDIX

To save time and money purchasing school supplies, bring along this list!

<table>
<tr><td>

BASIC MATERIALS AND TOOLS

- Alarm clock

- Audio recorder

- Dr. Lekura's Backpack Essentials (see next page)

- Binder clips

- Bins

- Calendars and planners

- Cloud platform

- Computer: consider multiple screens and/or larger screens

- Daily checklist (add the list you created in Chapter 3)

- External storage drive

- Extra essentials (add the list you created in Chapter 3)

- Notebooks

- Rubber bands

- Sticky notes

- Study apps

- Whiteboards

- Writing tools (highlighters, pencils, pens)

</td></tr>
</table>

Dr. Lekura's Backpack Essentials

<table>
<tr><td>

HEALTH CARE KIT
HAND SANITIZER

- Medicine for headaches, if needed
- Necessary prescriptions
- Artificial tears (for contact lens wearers)
- Band-Aids
- Medications
- Face mask/face shield

</td><td>

SCHOOL EQUIPMENT

- Extra highlighters and colored pens
- Binder clips
- Heavy-duty rubber bands
- Whiteout
- Extra paper
- Extra sticky notes
- Extra flashcards

</td></tr>
<tr><td>

ELECTRONICS

- Laptop
- Charger (for laptop & cellphone)
- Batteries AA/AAA
- Calculator
- Headphones/EarPods
- Recorder
- USB flash drive

</td><td>

OTHER

- Transportation pass
- Tissues
- Chapstick
- Water
- Snacks
- Extra cash or change for parking, tolls, and/or vending machines

</td></tr>
</table>

ABOUT THE AUTHOR

Dr. Erisaldi (Eri) Lekura is a graduate of Wayne State University in Detroit, Michigan, where he earned a bachelor's degree in Health Science. He received his Doctor of Optometry degree from Ferris State University's Michigan College of Optometry, in Big Rapids, Michigan. Dr. Lekura was on the Dean's List, was honored as a UMD Difference-Maker, and was also given recognition for Service Learning.

When he is not seeing patients, the author's hobbies include playing chess, beach volleyball, biking, and spending time outdoors. He also enjoys time with his family and friends and with his dog, Olive.

You can reach Dr. Lekura at **elekura@umich.edu**